A
REMARKABLE
LIFE

A
REMARKABLE
LIFE

Personal Experiences
from the Remarkable Life of
President Wilford Woodruff

Compiled by
Claire Ellen Koltko
Natalie Rose Ross
Michael Marsh

CFI
Springville, Utah

ISBN: 1-55517-925-8
e. 1

Published by CFI,
an imprint of Cedar Fort, Inc.
925 N. Springville, Utah, 84663
www.cedarfort.com

Distributed by:
CEDAR FORT

Cover design by Nicole Williams

Printed in the United States of America
10 9 8 7 6 5 4 3 2 1

Printed on acid-free paper

Contents

Preface

Wilford Woodruff was not just a prophet of God. He was also a husband, a missionary, and a Latter-day Saint who, during his ninety-one-year life span, witnessed many of the significant events in the early history of the Church. Fortunately for us, President Woodruff was also an avid journal writer who wrote about his experiences in each of these roles. He regarded his responsibility to record the miraculous events that he saw as a call from the Lord, and as a result, the Church archives contain thousands of pages of his journals and writings. Because he participated in many of the significant events of early Church history, his accounts contain invaluable records of these sacred events.

A Remarkable Life draws together scores of personal experiences collected from President Woodruff's writings. In compiling these accounts, we have standardized punctuation, spelling, and grammar. Amidst these changes, we have bracketed all words that were inserted to enhance clarity. These accounts not only provide an accurate record of the important events President Woodruff's witnessed, but they also serve to strengthen our testimonies, faith, and understanding of the gospel.

Acknowledgments

We would like to express our sincere gratitude to W. Jeffrey Marsh, our mentor and dear friend. Without him and his tireless efforts, this book would never have come to fruition.

Chapter 1

A Remarkable Life

Wilford Woodruff, the fourth president of The Church of Jesus Christ of Latter-day Saints, lived a remarkable and adventurous life. It became clear very early that he was destined for greatness and consequently much opposition from the adversary. It is literally a miracle that he survived childhood. "I have been numbered with those who are apparently the marked victims of misfortunes," observed Wilford Woodruff. "It has seemed to me at times as though some invisible power were watching my footsteps in search of an opportunity to destroy my life," which proved to be all too true (*Wilford Woodruff, His Life and Labors,* 5).

It is remarkable that President Woodruff survived to

adulthood, as any one of his many accidents could have easily proved fatal. He was preserved time and again by the grace of God. He wrote, "The repeated deliverances from all these remarkable dangers I ascribe to the mercies of my Heavenly Father" (*Wilford Woodruff, History of His Life and Labors,* 11).

The Adversary Seeks Wilford Woodruff's Life

Wilford Woodruff's inventory of life-threatening misfortunes is noteworthy, not only for the number of incidents but also for the broad variety of perils he faced. Of his many brushes with death, he wrote:

Varied and diverse are the lives and fortunes of men. While the paths of some are strewn with flowers and ease from the cradle to the grave, with naught to disturb their peace, others are marked victims of varied misfortunes, accidents, and dangers. The last-named class is the one in whose ranks I have stood through my infancy, childhood, youth, and manhood up to the present time; so much so, that it has seemed as though some invisible power or fate was watching my footsteps, in order to find some opportunity to take my life from the earth. I can only attribute the continuation of my life to the present time to a merciful God, whose hand has been stretched out and [who has] rescued me from death in the midst of the many dangers and hairbreadth escapes I have passed through, some of which I will here mention.

When three years of age, I fell into a caldron of boiling water, was instantly caught out, but was so badly scalded that it was nine months before I was considered out of danger.

At five years of age, I fell from the great beam of a barn, striking my face upon the floor, which came near breaking my neck.

Three months afterwards, I broke one of my arms, by falling down stairs. I soon after broke my other arm, by falling out of a high stoop upon a pile of timber.

When six years of age, I came near being killed by a surly bull. My father and I were feeding pumpkins to the cattle [when] a surly bull drove my cow away from the one she was eating. I took the pumpkin he had left, upon which he pitched at me. My father told me to throw down the pumpkin and run. I ran down a steep hill and took the pumpkin with me, being determined that the cow should have her rights. The bull pursued. As he was about to overtake me, I stepped into a posthole and fell; the bull leaped over me, after the pumpkin, and tore it to pieces with his horns, and would have served me in the same way had I not fallen.

During the same year, I went into my father's saw-mill, with several others. I got upon the head-block to take a ride, while the carriage was running back, not anticipating any danger. My leg was caught between the head-block and the fender-post, and broke both bones of my leg below the knee. I was taken to the house and lay nine hours before my bones were set, suffering severe pain; but, being young, my bones soon knit together, and I was upon my feet again. During my confinement by this lameness, my brother Thompson was also confined in the same room with the typhus fever.

When seven years of age, I was riding on the top of a load of hay which my uncle, Ozan Woodruff, was driving to the barn; he turned the load over upon me; I was nearly suffocated for the want of air, before the hay was removed.

At eight years old, I was riding in a one-horse wagon with several others. The horse took fright, ran down a steep hill, and turned the wagon over upon us; but again, while in the midst of danger, my life was preserved. None of us were seriously injured.

When nine years old, I climbed into an elm tree to obtain bark. I stepped upon a dry limb which broke, and I fell about fifteen feet, [landing] upon my back, which beat the breath out of my body. A cousin ran and told my parents I was dead. Before they arrived at the spot, I came to my senses, and met them.

When twelve years of age, I was drowned in Farmington River and sunk in thirty feet of water; and, after carrying one person to the bottom with me, I was miraculously saved by a young man named Bacon diving to the bottom, and carrying with him a large stone to hold him down until he obtained my body, not expecting to save me alive. I suffered much in being restored to life.

At thirteen years of age, while passing through Farmington meadows, in the depth of winter, the roads were drifted with snow; and in an exceedingly blustering day, I became so chilled and overcome with cold that I could not travel. I crawled into the hollow of a large apple tree. A man in the distance, seeing me go in, hastened to my rescue, realizing my danger more fully than I did. When he arrived at the spot, I had fallen asleep and was nearly insensible. He had much difficulty in arousing me to a sense of my situation. He procured means to carry me to my father's house, and through a kind providence, my life was again preserved.

At fourteen years of age, I split my left instep open with an ax, which went nearly through my foot; it was nine months getting well.

At fifteen years of age, I was bitten in my left hand by a mad dog in the last stage of hydrophobia. He dented my hand with his teeth but did not draw blood, and I was again preserved, through the mercies of God, from an awful death.

At the age of seventeen, I was riding a very ill-tempered horse that I was not acquainted with; and while going down a very steep rocky hill, the horse, taking advantage of the ground, suddenly leaped from the road and ran down the steep [hill], amid the rocks, at full speed. [He] commenced kicking up and attempted to throw me over his head upon the rocks; but I lodged upon the top of his head, grasped hold of each ear as with a death grip, expecting every moment to be dashed to pieces against the rocks. While in this position, sitting astride of his neck, with no bridle to guide him but his ears, he plunged down the hill under full speed, until he ran against a rock and was dashed to the ground. I went over both his head and the rocks, about one rod, and struck the ground square on my feet, [this] being the only thing visible that saved my life; for had I struck upon any other part of my body, it must have killed me instantly. As it was, my bones crushed from under me, as though they were reeds. It broke my left leg in two places and put out both my ankles in a shocking manner, and the horse came near rolling over me in his struggles to get up. My uncle, Titus Woodruff, saw me fall, got assistance, and carried me to his house. I lay from 2 p.m. until 10 without medical aid; then my father arrived, bringing Dr. Swift, of Farmington, with him, who set my bones, boxed up my limbs, and carried me in his carriage eight miles that night to my father's. My sufferings were very great. I had good attention, however, and in eight weeks I was outdoors upon my crutches.

In 1827, while attempting to clear the ice out of a waterwheel, standing upon the wheel with one arm around the shaft, a man hoisted the gate and let a full head of water upon it. As soon as the water struck the wheel it started. My feet slipped into the wheel, but I immediately plunged head foremost over the rim, into about three feet of water; and my weight drew my legs out of the wheel, or I should have been drawn under a shaft and crushed to death.

In 1831, while having charge of the flouring mill in Collinsville, Connecticut, I was standing inside of a breast wheel, twenty feet in diameter, upon one of the arms near the top, clearing out the ice, when a full head of water was let onto it. The wheel immediately started, but I dropped my ax and leaped through it to the bottom, by the shaft and arms, about twenty feet. As I struck the bottom of the wheel, I was rolled out against a ragged stone wall, with only about two feet [of] clearance between it and the wheel. The wheel caught me and rolled me out into the water below, where I found myself without any bones broken, but with some bruises and much fright.

During the winter of 1831, while in New Hartford, Connecticut, I passed through a severe course of lung fever.

In 1833, the day I was baptized, one of my horses, newly sharp shod, kicked my hat off my head, and had he struck two inches lower, would probably have killed me instantly. In ten minutes afterwards, while driving the same team down a hill, on a sleigh without any box, the bottom boards slipped forward under the roller and caught the ground, turned endwise, and fell on the horses' backs, throwing me between the horses. They ran to the bottom of the hill, dragging me with the lines, head foremost, with the sleigh on top of me, about twenty rods over a smooth snow path. I escaped unharmed, however, in the midst of both dangers.

In 1834, while traveling in Zion's Camp in Missouri, a rifle was accidentally discharged; and the ball passed through three tents, with about twelve men in each, and lodged in a wagon axletree, while a man was standing behind it, and injured no one. It passed within a few inches of my breast, and many others escaped as narrowly as myself.

A few months afterwards, a musket, heavily loaded with buckshot, was accidentally snapped within a few feet of me, with the muzzle pointed at my breast. It had a good flint and was well primed, but it [misfired], and my life was again preserved.

In April 1839, in Rochester, Illinois, I was riding upon the running gears of a wagon without a box, sitting upon the forward axletree, when the bolt fastening the coupling pole came out, which left the hind wheels;

and my weight on the forward bolster and tongue turned the coupling pole over on to the horses, turning the stakes upside down, and shut me up fast between the bolster and tongue, but in such a manner that my head and shoulders dragged on the ground. My horses took fright and ran out into an open prairie and dragged me in this position for about half a mile. I managed to guide them with my left hand, so as to run them into a corner of a high worm fence, where we landed in a pile together. I was considerably bruised but escaped without any broken bones.

July 23, 1842—President Joseph Smith [Jr.] sent me from Nauvoo to St. Louis, to procure a stock of paper. I went down upon a steamboat [and] was six days on the way, during which time I was severely attacked with bilious fever. The day I made my purchase, the fever was so high, I was scarcely sensible of what I was doing. As soon as I made my purchase and got my freight on board, I took my berth and lay there until I arrived at Nauvoo, on the 10th of August. I was confined to my bed forty days and passed through the most severe fit of sickness I ever endured; my life was despaired of by many of my friends. I was administered to by President [Joseph] Smith and the Twelve; my life was preserved by the power of God. I took a relapse twice after I began to recover; once, while in council with the Presidency and Twelve, my strength left me, my breath stopped, and I felt as though I was struck with death.

September 12, 1843—At five o'clock P.M., I left Boston on the express train for Portland. While passing through Chesterwoods, six miles south of Kennebunk, after dark, and while going at full speed, we struck one of the rails which some persons had raised by rolling a log under it, and landed in a pile. Three cars were filled with passengers, and their lives were saved by having a long train of freight between the passenger cars and the engine. All of [the freight cars] were mashed to pieces; the engineer was killed; some of the passengers had bones broken; I escaped unhurt.

On the 5th of October, 1846, while with the camp of Israel, building up Winter Quarters, on the west side of the Missouri River (then Indian country), I passed through one of the most painful and serious misfortunes of my life. I took my axe and went two and a half miles on to the bluffs, to cut some shingle timber to cover my cabin; I was accompanied by two men. While the third tree was falling, which was an oak, over two feet in diameter, I stepped behind it some ten feet and also to one side the same distance, where I thought I would be entirely out of danger. But when the tree fell, there being a crook in the body of it, which struck a knoll on the ground, the whole body shot endways back of the stump and bounded, and the butt of the tree struck me on the breast and knocked me several feet into the air against a standing oak. And the falling tree followed me in its bound and caught me against the standing tree, and I came down between them. Before reaching the earth, however, I was liberated from them, and struck the ground upon my feet, in a badly bruised condition. My left thigh, the whole length of it, and my hip, and left arm were much bruised; my breast bone and three ribs on my left side were broken; my lungs, vitals, and left side were also bruised in a shocking manner.

After the accident, I sat upon a log until Mr. John Garrison went a quarter of a mile to get my horse. Notwithstanding I was so badly hurt, I mounted my horse and rode two and a half miles over a very rough road, dismounting twice, in consequence of miry places. My breast and vitals were so badly torn to pieces that at each step of the horse the pain went through me like an arrow. I continued on horseback until I arrived at Turkey Creek, on the north side of Winter Quarters. I then became exhausted and was taken off my horse and carried to my wagon in a chair. I was met in the street by Presidents Brigham Young, [Heber] C. Kimball, and [Willard] Richards and others, who assisted in carrying me to my family. Before laying me upon my bed, the Presidency laid hands upon me, rebuked my suffering and distress in the name of the Lord, and said I should live and not die. I was then laid upon my bed in my wagon, and as the Apostles prophesied upon my head, so it came to pass. I employed no physician on this occasion, but was administered to by the elders of Israel and nursed by my wife. I lay upon my bed unable to move until my breastbone began to knit together, which commenced on the ninth day. I began to walk about in twenty days; in thirty days from the time I was hurt, I again commenced to do hard labor. . . .

On the 21st day of April, 1856, while assisting to remove an ox that had died from poison and had been skinned, I inoculated my arm with poison, and mortification ensued. The poison worked through my system for seven days before it showed itself outwardly. On the 28th, my arm began to swell, was in great pain, and showed signs of mortification. I showed it to President [Brigham] Young, who advised me to cleanse my stomach immediately and put on onion poultices and anything that would draw the poison from my system into my arm, which counsel I immediately put in execution. The 29th was another trying day to my life; the poison had so thoroughly penetrated my whole system, that my strength left me. I could not stand, I was led to my bed, my bowels and stomach ceased to act, my speech was like that of a drunken man. President [Brigham] Young called, in company with Dr. Sprague, and laid hands upon me, and rebuked the disease and the power of the destroyer which had seized my body, and promised me in the name of the Lord that I should not die, but live to finish my work which was appointed me upon the earth. I soon began to recover. The poison and mortification left my system and centered in my arm and was drawn from my arm, through the aid of charcoal poultices; moistened with a strong decoction of wormwood, ragweed, and wild sage; the dead flesh was removed from my arm with instruments and lunar caustic; and in a few days, I was well again.

I have occupied considerable space in referring to those peculiar circumstances which have attended me during life, and to sum the matter up, it stands thus: I have broken both legs—one in two places—both arms, my breastbone, and three ribs, and had both ankles dislocated. I have been drowned, frozen, scalded, and bit by a mad dog; have been in two waterwheels under full head of water; have passed through several severe fits of sickness, and encountered poison in its worst forms; have landed in a pile of railroad ruins; have barely been missed by passing bullets; and have passed through a score of other hairbreadth escapes.

It has appeared miraculous to me, that with all the injuries and broken bones which I have had, I have not a lame limb but have been enabled to endure the hardest labor, exposures, and journeys—have often walked forty, fifty, and on one occasion, sixty miles in a day. The protection and mercy of God has been over me, and my life thus far has been preserved; for which blessings I feel to render the gratitude of my heart to my Heavenly Father, praying that the remainder of my days may be spent in his service and in the building up of his kingdom. ("History of Wilford Woodruff," *Millennial Star* 27: 359–60, 374–76, 391–92)

The Importance of Written Records

In pondering why his life had to be so miraculously preserved on so many occasions, President Woodruff concluded the following as a possible explanation:

The devil has sought to take away my life from the day I was born. I seem to be a marked victim of the adversary. I can find but one reason for this: the devil knew if I got into the Church of Jesus Christ of Latter-day Saints, I would write the history of that Church and leave on record the works and teachings of the prophets, of the apostles and elders. Whenever I heard Joseph Smith preach, teach, or prophesy, I always felt it my duty to write it; I felt uneasy and could not eat, drink, or sleep until I did write. (*Wilford Woodruff's Journal*, 7:55; January 20, 1872)

The Prophet Joseph Smith taught that "the nearer a person approaches the Lord, a greater power will be manifested by the adversary to prevent the accomplishment of His purposes" (Life of Heber C. Kimball, 132). Certainly, the adversary knew of Wilford Woodruff's grand mission and potential and that he would disrupt the evil designs that plotted against the work of God.

Chapter 2

Strength of Character

Wilford Woodruff was born in Farmington, Connecticut, in 1807, to Aphek and Beulah Thompson Woodruff. He learned the trade of flour miller in the gristmills of Farmington. When he was twenty-five years old, he moved to Oswego County, New York, where he purchased a farm. There he heard the message of the Mormon missionaries for the first time and believed their testimonies of the marvelous restoration of the gospel, through the Prophet Joseph Smith. He was baptized on December 31, 1833, just two days after first hearing the Mormon missionaries preach.

From the time he was baptized until his death sixty-five years later at the age of ninety, he was one of the most devoted and energetic missionaries in the Church. In 1839, at the age of thirty-two, he was ordained one of the Twelve Apostles. In 1889, at age eighty-two, he was called as the fourth president of The Church of Jesus Christ of Latter-day Saints. Because his life extended through most of the nineteenth century (1807–1898), he participated in many of the major events that helped lay the foundation of the restored kingdom of God.

A Legacy of Hard Work

He possessed an incredible work ethic, which he inherited from the example of his parents and grandparents. His great-grandfather Josiah Woodruff lived to almost one hundred years of age and performed manual labor up to the time of his death. His grandfather Eldad Woodruff had a similar reputation for hard work. His father, Aphek Woodruff, was known for working eighteen-hour days. From the examples of these men, Wilford learned early in life to work hard. "He seemed to be interested in every phase of human activity. 'We find him,' writes Elder [Matthias F. Cowley], 'grubbing willows, breaking land, digging ditches, constructing roads, barns, and homes. He was indeed a model of industry. All honorable work was God's work, whether he dug a ditch, preached a sermon or wrote a history'" (*The Presidents of the Church,* 125–26).

Further describing Wilford Woodruff's strength of character, Elder Cowley commented on his activities during 1862:

"It is wonderful how Wilford Woodruff busied himself in a multitude of occupations. His journal furnishes evidence of a remarkably busy life. One moment he was recording stirring events in the history of the world; then he is writing Church History; the next moment tells something of a correspondence received from those who desire information concerning the Latter-day Saints. The next page contains an account of his orchard and the work of planting more fruit trees; later he is found in the irrigation furrows; then he is addressing missionaries upon their duties and responsibilities; on the same page he opens a prophetic inspiration of his soul and tells of things to come. In all he sees the glory and goodness of God. He listens to the words of the Prophet and makes careful record of them. Then he discourses upon the principles of a free government and the rights of a people under a constitution" (*The Presidents of the Church,* 125).

Marriage to Phoebe Carter

Wilford Woodruff met Phoebe Carter in Kirtland, Ohio, in 1837. The couple had known each other for only two and a half months when they decided to marry. Frederick G. Williams, counselor in the First Presidency, performed the marriage ceremony in the Prophet Joseph Smith's home on April 13, 1837. Wilford and Phoebe were husband and wife for forty-eight years, until her death in 1885.

Some of the major highlights from the remarkable life of Wilford Woodruff are listed are the following pages.

Highlights from the Life of Wilford Woodruff

Year	Age	Event
1807		Born at Farmington, Hartford County, Connecticut (March 1) to Aphek and Beulah Thompson Woodruff.
1821	14	Sent to live with Col. George Cowles to learn the trade of miller.
1832	25	First learns of the "Mormons" through a newspaper article. Moves with his brother Azmon to Rushland, Oswego County, New York, to purchase a farm.
1833	26	Elders Zera Pulsipher and Elijah Cheney call at the Woodruff farm in Rushland (December 29). Wilford is baptized a member of The Church of Jesus Christ of Latter-day Saints by Elder Zera Pulsipher (December 31) near Richmond, New York.
1834	27	Meets Joseph Smith and participates in Zion's Camp (May–July).
1834	27	Ordained a priest at Adam-ondi-Ahman, by Simeon Carter (November 5).

1835	28	Ordained an elder by Warren Parrish, near Memphis, Tennessee (April 4).
1834–6	27–29	Serves a mission to the Southern states.
1836	29	While on his mission to the Southern states, he learns from David W. Patten that he has been called to membership in the Second Quorum of Seventy (April 21). Ordained a seventy by David W. Patten and Warren Parrish (May 31). Called and ordained to the First Quorum of Seventy at Kirtland (December 20), taking his place January 3, 1837.
1837	30	Marries Phoebe Carter (April 13). Receives patriarchal blessing from Joseph Smith Sr. (April 15). Leaves Kirtland for a mission to the Eastern states and the Fox Islands, off the coast of Maine (May 14).
1838	31	Called to the Quorum of the Twelve by revelation to the Prophet Joseph Smith (July 8).

1839	32	Ordained an apostle by Brigham Young at the temple site in Far West, Missouri (April 26). Leaves home in Montrose, Iowa, for a two-year mission to England with the Twelve Apostles (August 8), arriving in New York City (November 8) and sailing for Liverpool (December 19).
1840	33	Arrives at Liverpool (January 11), going first to Preston, then laboring in Staffordshire. Arrives at the home of John Benbow, Ledbury, Herefordshire (March 4), and baptizes about six hundred people in the next thirty-eight days. Goes to London (August 11).
1841	34	Helps secure copyright to Book of Mormon at Stationer's Hall, London, in the name of Joseph Smith Jr. (February 8). Sails for the United States with Brigham Young and six additional members of the Twelve (April 20). Arrives in New York (May 20).
1842	35	Hauls stone for the Nauvoo Temple (January).

1843–44	36	Appointed to a mission in the Eastern states to raise funds for the Nauvoo Temple (April 19), leaves (July 7), arrives in Philadelphia (August 5), and returns to Nauvoo (November 4).
1844	37	Moves into a new home in Nauvoo (March 4). Leaves shortly thereafter for another mission to the Eastern states. Has a short stay in Michigan (June 1). Arrives in Boston (June 26), where he sees press account of the June 27 murder of Joseph Smith. Leaves for Nauvoo (July 20), arriving with other members of the Twelve (August 6). Attends the special conference in Nauvoo sustaining Brigham Young and the Twelve Apostles (August 8). Chosen to preside over the European Mission (August 12), leaves Nauvoo (on August 28), and sails from New York (December 8).
1845	38	Arrives at Liverpool (January 3), stays one year, returns to New York City (March 6, 1846).
1846	39	Arrives in Nauvoo from his European mission (April 13) and

		finds that the exodus had begun in February. Dedicates the Nauvoo Temple with Orson Hyde (April 30). Leaves Nauvoo (May 16) to join the pioneers and arrives at Mount Pisgah (June 15).
1847	40	Enters Salt Lake Valley, conveying President Brigham Young in his wagon (July 24). Returns with Brigham Young to Winter Quarters (August 26). Arrives at Winter Quarters (October 31).
1848	41	Leaves Winter Quarters on a mission to gather the Eastern Saints (June 21). Presides over the Church in the Eastern states.
1850	43	Leaves New York with a company of Saints for the West (April 9).
1851	44	Appointed to the Utah territorial legislature.
1856	49	Appointed as a historian for the Church (April 7).
1867	60	Participates in the reestablishment of a School of the Prophets in Salt Lake City (December 16).

1877	70	Offers a dedicatory prayer for the St. George Temple and is appointed as temple president (January). Is baptized for the signers of the American Declaration of Independence in the St. George Temple (August 21). Goes to Salt Lake City for the funeral of President Brigham Young (August).
1879	72	While in Arizona to escape persecution under the antipolygamy act (February), does missionary work among the Indians.
1880	73	Sustained as president of the Quorum of the Twelve Apostles (October 6).
1881	74	Appointed superintendent of the Y. M. M. I. A. (January).
1885	78	Suffers in exile due to persecution against plural marriage resulting from the Edmunds Act.
1887	80	Watches funeral procession of President John Taylor from windows of the historian's office (July 17). Leads the Church as president of

		the Quorum of the Twelve Apostles after John Taylor's death.
1888	81	Dedicates the Manti Temple (17 May).
1889	82	Sustained as president of the Church (April 7).
1890	83	Issues Manifesto announcing the end of plural marriage (written September 24 and accepted by Church membership October 6).
1893	86	Dedicates the Salt Lake Temple (April 6).
1894	87	Organizes the Utah Genealogical Society (November).
1896	89	Changes fast day observance from the first Thursday to first Sunday of each month (November 5).
1897	90	Attends public celebration of his ninetieth birthday (March 1). Records his testimony on a "talking machine."
1898	91	Makes last public appearance in

Salt Lake City at dedication of Pioneer Park (July 24). Dies in San Francisco, California (September 2). Is laid to rest in the Salt Lake City Cemetery.

"God has no respect for persons in this priesthood any further than as they magnify their callings and do their duty" (*Discourses of Wilford Woodruff,* 298). Wilford Woodruff not only spoke these words but also exemplified them.

Chapter 3

Conversion and Commitment to the Gospel

As a young boy, Wilford Woodruff not only read but also loved the Bible. He desired to see an apostle of the Lord Jesus Christ someday. He later walked with prophets and was himself called as an apostle and then as the prophet, seer, and revelator of the Lord. His greatest desire and chief concern in life was to serve the Lord and remain faithful in all things to the end of his life. In a revelation given through the Prophet Joseph Smith, the Lord referred to Wilford Woodruff as "my servant" (D&C 118:6). No greater tribute could be paid to this humble servant of God.

Searches for the Truth

At an early age my mind was exercised upon religious subjects, although I never made a profession until 1830. I did not then join any church, for the reason that I could not find any denomination whose doctrines, faith or practice, agreed with the gospel of Jesus Christ, or the ordinances and gifts which the Apostles taught. Although the ministers of the day taught that the faith, gifts, graces, miracles and ordinances, which the ancient Saints enjoyed, were done away and no longer needed, I did not believe it to be true, only as they were done away through the unbelief of the children of men. I believed the same gifts, graces, miracles and power would be manifest in one age of the world as in another, when God had a church upon the earth, and that the Church of God would be reestablished upon the earth, and that I should live to see it. ("History of Wilford Woodruff," *Millennial Star* 27:182)

Keeps "Aloof from all Professions"

I attended the meetings, inquiry, Sunday schools, and prayer meetings. I tried to get religion by effort and prayer, but my efforts created darkness instead of light and I was not happy in the attempt. They wanted us to give our hearts to God without telling us what to do or explaining any principle in a comprehensive manner. There were many young people at that time of my age who made a profession of religion. I did not wish to make a mockery of sacred things by professing light when I had received none, so I kept aloof from all professions. (*Wilford Woodruff, His Life and Labors,* 21–22)

An Avid Reader of the Bible and a Seeker after Truth

The Lord blessed me with joy and happiness such as I had never before enjoyed, doubtless because I was living up to the best light I had. I had no apostle or prophet to teach me the right way; so I had to do the best I could. In my zeal to promote good, I got up prayer meetings in our village and prayed for light and knowledge. It was my desire to receive the ordinances of the gospel, as I could plainly see by reading the Bible that baptism by immersion was a sacred ordinance. In my eagerness, yet being ignorant of the holy priesthood and of the true authority to officiate in the ordinances of eternal life, I requested the Baptist minister to baptize me. At first he refused because I told him I would not join his church as it did not harmonize with the apostolic church which our Savior established. Finally after several conversations, he baptized me on the 5th of May, 1831. He also baptized my brother Asahel. This was the first and only gospel ordinance I sought for until I joined the Church of Jesus Christ of Latter-day Saints. (In "A Place of Prayer," *Improvement Era* 25, no. 4 [February 1922], 383)

Finds Answers in the Bible

After praying very earnestly on one occasion to know if any group of people on earth represented the Lord, Wilford recorded:

The Spirit of the Lord said unto me: "Go to my Word and I will there show thee my will and answer thy prayer." I opened the Bible promiscuously, praying the Lord to direct me to that portion of his Word which would answer my prayer. I opened to the 56th Chapter of Isaiah. I was satisfied it was in response to my prayer. I felt that the salvation of God was about to be revealed and His righteousness come forth. I was also satisfied that I should live to see the people of God gathered. From this time on until the gospel found me I was contented and felt that I should trouble myself no more about the churches and the ministers. (*Wilford Woodruff, His Life and Labors,* 29)

Gains an Understanding of the Purpose of Life

I was twenty-three years of age; and in reflecting upon the past, I became sincerely convinced that there was no real peace of mind or true happiness except in the service of God and in doing those things which would meet His approval. As far as my imagination would enable me, I brought before my mind all the honor, glory, and happiness of the whole world. I thought of the gold and the wealth of the rich, of the glory, grandeur, and power of kings, presidents, princes, and rulers. I thought of the military renown of Alexander, Napoleon, and other great generals. I cast my mind over the innumerable paths through which the giddy world travels in search of pleasure and happiness. In summing up the whole matter in the vision of my mind, I had to exclaim with Solomon: "All is vanity of vanities sayeth the preacher."

I could see that within a few years all would end alike in the grave. I was convinced that no man could enjoy true happiness and obtain that which would feed the immortal soul, except God was his friend and Jesus Christ his advocate. I was convinced that man became their friend by doing the will of the Father, and by keeping His commandments. I made a firm resolution that from then I would seek the Lord to know His will, to keep His commandments, and to follow the dictates of His Holy Spirit. Upon this ground I was determined to stand and to spend my future life in the maintenance of these convictions. (*Wilford Woodruff, His Life and Labors,* 26–27)

Believes Missionaries and Is Baptized

When Wilford Woodruff heard the witness of two Mormon missionaries on December 29, 1833, he quickly recognized the truth of their message and was baptized just two days later.

In the winter of 1833, and on the twenty-ninth day of December, there came to his home two humble elders of The Church of Jesus Christ of Latter-day Saints. They were Zera Pulsipher and Elijah Cheney. At the time of their appearance, [Wilford] and his brother Azmon were away from the house engaged in their daily labors; but Azmon's wife knew very well the frame of mind, both of her husband and his brother Wilford. Their hopes and expectations had been the subject of conversation in their humble home. She therefore received the elders kindly and gave them to understand that her husband and his brother would be anxious to hear them preach.

According to the custom of the Mormon elders then . . . a meeting was appointed at the schoolhouse and notices were circulated throughout the village. The story of this new experience is told by Wilford Woodruff in a simple and beautiful manner. (*Wilford Woodruff, His Life and Labors*, 32–33)

Upon my arrival home my sister-in-law informed me of the meeting. I immediately turned out my horses and started for the schoolhouse without waiting for supper. On my way I prayed most sincerely that the Lord would give me his spirit, and that if these men were the servants of God I might know it, and that my heart might be prepared to receive the divine message they had to deliver.

When I reached the place of meeting, I found the house already packed. My brother Azmon was there before I arrived. He was equally eager to hear what these men had to say. I crowded my way through the assembly and seated myself upon one of the writing desks where I could see and hear everything that took place.

Elder Pulsipher opened with prayer. He knelt down and asked the Lord in the name of Jesus Christ for what he wanted. His manner of prayer and the influence which went with it impressed me greatly. The spirit of the Lord rested upon me and bore witness that he was a servant of God. After singing, he preached to the people for an hour and a half.

The spirit of God rested mightily upon him, and he bore a strong testimony of the divine authenticity of the Book of Mormon and of the mission of the Prophet Joseph Smith. I believed all that he said. The spirit bore witness of its truth. Elder Cheney then arose and added his testimony to the truth of the words of Elder Pulsipher.

Liberty was then given by the elders to any one in

the congregation to arise and speak for or against what they had heard as they might choose. Almost instantly I found myself upon my feet. The spirit of the Lord urged me to bear testimony of the truth of the message delivered by these elders. I exhorted my neighbors and friends not to oppose these men, for they were the true servants of God. They had preached to us that night the pure gospel of Jesus Christ. When I sat down, my brother Azmon arose and bore a similar testimony. He was followed by several others. (In "Conversions through the Book of Mormon," *Improvement Era* 63, no. 11 [November 1960], 814)

Commits Himself to the Lord

From the moment Wilford Woodruff determined to join the Church, there was no turning back. He wrote:

I felt that I could truly exclaim with the prophet of God, "I had rather be a door-keeper in the house of my God than to dwell in the tents of wickedness." The fulness of the everlasting gospel had come at last. It filled my heart with great joy. It laid the foundation of a greater and more glorious work than I ever expected to see in this life. I pray God in the name of Jesus Christ to guide my future life, that I may live to His honor and glory, and be a blessing to my fellowmen, and in the end be saved in His celestial kingdom, even so, Amen. (*Wilford Woodruff, His Life and Labors,* 36)

Has Conviction that Jesus Is the Christ

At an early age my mind began to be exercised upon

religious subjects, but I never made a profession of religion until 1830 when I was twenty-three years of age. I did not then join any church for the reason that I could not find a body of people, denomination, or church that had for its doctrine, faith, and practices those principles, ordinances, and gifts which constituted the gospel of Jesus Christ as taught by Him and His apostles. Neither did I find anywhere the manifestations of the Holy Ghost with its attendant gifts and graces. When I conversed with the ministers of the various denominations or sects, they would always tell me that prophets, apostles, revelations, healing, etc., were given to establish Jesus Christ and His doctrine, but that they have ever since been done away with because no longer needed in the Church and kingdom of God. Such a declaration I never could and never would believe. I did believe, however, that revelation, the gifts and graces, and the faith once delivered to the Saints—a faith which they have enjoyed in all ages when God has had an acknowledged people on the earth—could be done away with only through the disobedience and unbelief of the children of men. I believed every gift, office, and blessing to be just as necessary now to constitute the true Church of Christ and kingdom of God as in any age of the world.

This belief was firmly fixed upon my mind for two reasons: first, from the study of the Bible I found that the principle of cause and effect was the same in all ages, and that the divine promises made were to all generations. At the same time, I found no changes in the gospel in the days of Christ and the apostles, or that there would be any change in the plan of salvation in the last days.

I learned also from the Scriptures that many of the ancient prophets, that Christ and His apostles foresaw by inspiration and revelation that the Gentile nations would apostatize and turn away from the true faith and from the Church and kingdom of God as the Jews had anciently done; that there would be a falling away from the apostolic faith, from its doctrines and ordinances; that other systems would arise; that when these false systems should reach their fullness, the God of heaven would set up His Kingdom; that an angel would restore the gospel; and that it should be preached in all the world for a witness before the Savior should come to reign. I further believed that the gospel had been taken from the Jews and given to the Gentiles; that the Gentiles had, as foretold by the prophets, fallen into apostasy; and that in the last days Israel should be restored and the promises concerning that people should be fulfilled. All these things I learned from the Scriptures and they made a lasting impression upon my mind. (*Wilford Woodruff, His Life and Labors,* 14–15)

Teachings of Robert Mason Help Direct Wilford's Search for Truth

The second reason for my peculiar belief in such principles, teachings, and doctrines was that in the days of my youth I was taught by an aged man named Robert Mason, who lived in Sainsbury, Connecticut. By many he was called a prophet; to my knowledge, many of his prophecies have been fulfilled. The sick were healed by him through the laying on of hands in the name of Jesus Christ, and devils were cast out. His son was a raving maniac. After praying and fasting for him nine days, he arose on the ninth day and commanded in the name of Jesus Christ the devil to come out of him. The devil obeyed and the boy was made whole from that very hour. This man instilled these principles into my mind as well as into the mind of my oldest brother Azmon.

Father Mason did not claim that he had any authority to officiate in the ordinances of the gospel, nor did he believe that such authority existed on the earth. He did believe, however, that it was the privilege of any man who had faith in God to fast and pray for the healing of the sick by the laying on of hands. He believed it his right and the right of every honest-hearted man or woman to receive light and knowledge, visions, and revelations by the prayer of faith. He told me that the day was near when the Lord would establish His Church and Kingdom upon the earth with all its ancient gifts and blessings. He said that such a work would commence upon the earth before he died, but that he would not live to partake of its blessings. He said that I should live to do so, and that I should become a conspicuous actor in that kingdom.

The last time I ever saw him he related to me the following vision which he had in his field in open day: "I was carried away in a vision and found myself in the midst of a vast orchard of fruit trees. I became hungry and wandered through this vast orchard searching for fruit to eat, but I found none. While I stood in amazement finding no fruit in the midst of so many trees, they began to fall to the ground as if torn up by a whirlwind. They continued to fall until there was not a tree standing in the whole orchard. I immediately saw thereafter shoots springing up from the roots and forming themselves into young and beautiful trees. These budded, blossomed, and brought forth fruit which ripened and was the most beautiful to look upon of anything my eyes had ever beheld. I stretched forth my hand and plucked some of the fruit. I gazed upon it with delight; but when I was about to eat of it, the vision closed and I did not taste the fruit.

"At the close of the vision I bowed down in humble prayer and asked the Lord to show me the meaning of the vision. Then the voice of the Lord came to me saying: 'Son of man, thou hast sought me diligently to know the truth concerning my Church and Kingdom among men. This is to show you that my Church is not organized among men in the generation to which you belong; but in the days of your children the Church and kingdom of God shall be made manifest with all the gifts and the blessings enjoyed by the Saints in past ages. You shall live to be made acquainted with it, but shall not partake of its blessings before you depart this life. You will be blest of the Lord after death because you have followed the dictation of my Spirit in this life.'"

When Father Mason had finished relating the vision and its interpretation, he said, calling me by my Christian name: "Wilford, I shall never partake of this fruit in the flesh, but you will and you will become a conspicuous actor in the new kingdom." He then turned and left me. These were the last words he ever spoke to me upon the earth. To me this was a very striking circumstance. I had passed many days during a period of twenty years with this old Father Mason. He had never mentioned this vision to me before. On this occasion he said he felt impelled by the Spirit of the Lord to relate it to me.

The vision was given to him about the year 1800. He related it to me in 1830, the spring in which the Church was organized. Three years later when I was baptized into the Church of Jesus Christ of Latter-day Saints, almost the first person I thought of was this prophet, Robert Mason. Upon my arrival in Missouri with Zion's Camp, I wrote him a long letter in which I informed him that I had found the true gospel with all its blessings; that the authority of the Church of Christ had been restored to the earth as he had told me it would be; that I had received the ordinances of baptism and the laying on of hands; that I knew for myself that God had established through Joseph Smith, the Prophet, the Church of Christ upon the earth.

He received my letter with great joy and had it read over to him many times. He handled it as he had handled the fruit in the vision. He was very aged and soon died without having the privilege of receiving the ordinances of the gospel at the hands of an elder of the Church.

The first opportunity I had after the truth of baptism for the dead was revealed, I went forth and was baptized for him in the temple font at Nauvoo. He was a good man, a true prophet; for his prophecies have been fulfilled. There was so much reason in the teachings of this man, and such harmony between them and the prophecies and teachings of Christ and of the apostles and prophets of old, that I believed in them with all my heart. (*Wilford Woodruff, His Life and Labors,* 15–18)

On another occasion Wilford Woodruff described the influence Robert Mason had on him:

When I was a boy, there was an old man who used to visit at my father's house. His name was Robert Mason, and I heard teachings from him from the time that I was eight years old and upwards, and they were teachings that I shall ever remember. And he taught my father's household many important truths concerning the church and kingdom of God, and told them many things in relation to the prophets and the things that were coming upon the earth. But his teachings were received by but few. They were unpopular with the Christian world, but nearly all who did receive his teachings have joined the Latter-day Saints.

Prophets were not popular in that day any more than now, and I have often thought of many things which the old man taught me in the days of my youth since I received the fulness of the gospel and became a member of the Church of Christ.

He said, "When you read the Bible, do you ever think that what you read there is going to be fulfilled? The teachers of the day," said he, "spiritualize the Bible, but when you read in the Bible about the dreams, visions, revelations and predictions of Ezekiel, Isaiah, Jeremiah, or any other of the prophets or apostles, relative to the gathering of Israel and the building up of Zion, . . . you may understand that it means just what it says, and that it will be fulfilled upon the earth in the last days. And when you read of men laying hands upon the sick and healing them, and casting out devils and working miracles in the name of Jesus Christ, it means what it says." And he further said, "The church of Christ and kingdom of God is not upon the earth, but it has been taken from the children of men through unbelief and because they have taken away from the gospel some of its most sacred ordinances, and have instituted in their stead forms and ceremonies without the power of God, and have turned from the truth unto fables; but," said he, "it will soon be restored again unto the children of men upon the earth, with its ancient gifts and powers, for the scriptures cannot be fulfilled without it. I shall not live to see it, but," said he to me, "you will live to see that day, and you will become a conspicuous actor in that kingdom, and when you see that day, then that which the prophets have spoken will be fulfilled."

I did not join any church, believing that the church of Christ in its true organization did not exist upon the earth. But when the principles of the everlasting gospel were first proclaimed unto me, I believed it with all my heart, and was baptized the first sermon I heard, for the Spirit of God bore testimony to me in power that it was true.

And I believe that I should never have joined any church had I not heard the fulness of the gospel. I was greatly blessed in receiving it, and was filled with joy unspeakable, and I have never been sorry but I have rejoiced all the day long. . . . I thought of the teaching and words of the old prophet Mason, for he came the nearest to being a true prophet of God in his predictions and works of any man I ever saw, until I saw men administering in the Holy Priesthood.

"But," said he, "I have no right to administer in the ordinances of the gospel, neither has any man unless he receives it by revelation from God out of heaven, as did the ancients. But if my family or friends are sick, I have the right to lay hands upon them, and pray for them in the name of Jesus Christ. And if we can get faith to be healed, it is our privilege." And I will here say that many were healed through his faith and prayers. (*Journal of Discourses,* 4:99–100)

Consecrates His All to the Lord

On December 31, 1834, Wilford entered into the law of consecration, consecrating all his time, talents, and earthly possessions to the Lord.

Believing it to be the duty of the Latter-day Saints to consecrate and dedicate all their property, with themselves, unto God in order to become lawful heirs to the celestial kingdom of God, I therefore, with this view, consecrated all I had (though but little) before Edward Partridge, the Presiding Bishop of the Church, in Clay County, Missouri, in this form: "Be it known that I, Wilford Woodruff, do freely covenant with my God, that I freely consecrate and dedicate myself, together with all my properties and effects, unto the Lord, for the purpose of assisting in the building up of His Kingdom and His Zion upon the earth, that I may keep His law. I lay all before the Bishop of His Church, that I may be a lawful heir to the celestial kingdom of God." (*Wilford Woodruff's Journal,* 1:16; December 31, 1834)

Sacrifices to Help Build the Kingdom of God

It would be difficult to find another person in the nineteenth century who sacrificed more to help build up the kingdom of God on the earth than Wilford Woodruff. Once Wilford put his hand to the plow, he never looked back. From his journals, near the close of his life, he penned a brief summary of his sacrifices and experiences:

From the beginning of my ministry in 1834 until the close of 1895 I have traveled in all 172,369 miles; held 7,655 meetings; preached 3,526 discourses; organized 51 branches of the Church and 77 preaching places; my journeys cover England, Scotland, Wales, and 23 states and 5 territories of the Union. My life abounds in incidents which to me surely indicate the direct interposition of God whom I firmly believe has guided my every step. On 27 distinct occasions I have been saved from dangers which threatened my life. (*Wilford Woodruff's Journal*, 9:407; June 12, 1896)

Desires the Blessings of Eternity above All Earthly Blessings

It is better for us to fall in defense of truth, than to deny the words of God, and go to hell. It is better to suffer stripes for the testimony of Christ, than to suffer and fall by our sins and transgressions, and then to have to suffer afterwards. I would rather seal my testimony with my blood, and lay my body to rest in the grave, and have my spirit go to the other side of the veil, to enjoy a long eternity of light, truth, blessings, and knowledge which the Lord will bestow upon every man who keeps his law, than to spend a few short years of earthly pleasure, and be deprived of those blessings, and the society of my friends and brethren behind the veil. (*Journal of Discourses*, 2:199)

Sees the Destiny of the Restored Gospel

This is the only dispensation which God has ever established that was foreordained, before the world was made, not to be overcome by wicked men and devils. . . . The prophet [Enoch] asked the Lord whether there would ever be a time when the earth should rest; and the Lord answered that in the dispensation of the fulness of times the earth would fill the measure of its days, and then it would rest from wickedness and abominations, for in that day he would establish his kingdom upon it, to be thrown down no more for ever. Then a reign of righteousness would commence and the honest and meek of the earth would be gathered together to serve the Lord, and upon them would rest power to build up the great Zion of God in the latter days. . . .

This dispensation is one that all the patriarchs and prophets had their eye upon, and the Lord has commenced it, and has carried it on. . . .

The work that is to be so marvelous in the eyes of men has already commenced, and is assuming shape and proportions; but they cannot see it. It will consist in preaching the gospel to all the world, gathering the Saints from the midst of all those nations who reject it; building up the Zion of God; establishing permanently in the earth his kingdom; preparing for the work of the gathering of the Jews and the events that will follow their settlement in their own lands, and in preparing for ourselves holy places in which to stand when the judgments of God shall overtake the nations. This is truly a good work. (*The Discourses of Wilford Woodruff*, 109–11)

Chosen in the Premortal Life

When President Joseph F. Smith received a vision of the post-earthly spirit world, he saw that Wilford Woodruff was one of those chosen in the premortal life to lead the Church in this final dispensation:

The Prophet Joseph Smith, and my father, Hyrum Smith, Brigham Young, John Taylor, Wilford Woodruff, and other choice spirits who were reserved to come forth in the fulness of times to take part in laying the foundations of the great latter-day work. . . .

[These men] were also among the noble and great ones who were chosen in the beginning to be rulers in the Church of God.

Even before they were born, they, with many others, received their first lessons in the world of spirits and were prepared to come forth in the due time of the Lord to labor in his vineyard for the salvation of the souls of men. (D&C 138:53, 55–56)

Phoebe Woodruff Sacrifices for the Gospel

Phoebe Carter Woodruff, wife of Wilford Woodruff, was no less committed to the gospel of Jesus Christ. She records the pain of separation from her family because of her con-

version to the gospel, when she chose to cast her lot with the Latter-day Saints:

In the year 1834, I embraced the Gospel, as revealed through the Prophet Joseph Smith, and, about a year after, I left my parents and kindred, and journeyed to Kirtland, Ohio, a distance of one thousand miles, a lone maid, sustained only by my faith and trust in Israel's God. My friends marvelled at my course, as did I, but something within impelled me on. My mother's grief at my leaving home was almost more than I could bear; and had it not been for the spirit within I should have faltered at the last. My mother told me she would rather see me buried than going thus alone into the heartless world, and especially was she concerned about my leaving home to cast my lot among the Mormons. "Phoebe," she said, impressively, "will you come back to me if you find Mormonism false?" I answered thrice, "Yes, mother, I will."

These were my words well remembered to this day; she knew I would keep my promise. My answer relieved her trouble; but it cost us all much sorrow to part. When the time came for my departure I dared not trust myself to say farewell, so I wrote my good-bye to each, and leaving them on my table, ran down stairs and jumped into the carriage. Thus I left my beloved home of childhood to link my life with the Saints of God. (*Representative Women of Deseret,* 35–36)

Phoebe married Wilford Woodruff in 1837. Their first child was born in 1838 at her parents' home. Wilford was serving a mission in the area at the time. Her parents pled with her to remain with them, for the sake of the child, but she and Wilford journeyed to Nauvoo to be with the Saints.

*Their little girl died at Nauvoo in 1840. (*Wilford Woodruff, His Life and Labors, *93–98, 152)*

*The strength of Phoebe's testimony had a great impact on her family. A short time later, Wilford Woodruff was able to baptize both Phoebe's mother and father. (*Representative Women of Deseret, *39)*

Chapter 4

A Marvelous Missionary

President Woodruff served four separate missions during his life and spent many other years sharing the gospel he loved. During his missions, Wilford Woodruff labored without purse or scrip. On his first mission to the Southern States, he was a priest in the Aaronic Priesthood until Warren Parrish ordained him an elder near Memphis, Tennessee, on April 4, 1835.

Wilford had only been married a month in 1837 when he departed for a second mission to the Eastern States and then the Fox Islands. While he was serving, more than one hundred people in the Fox Islands joined the Church. Shortly after returning, he was able to baptize his father, stepmother, and several other relatives.

When he returned to Illinois, he came with ten wagons full of converts.

In August 1838, while laboring in the Fox Islands, Elder Woodruff learned in a letter from Thomas B. Marsh that he had been called by revelation to fill one of the vacancies in the Quorum of the Twelve. He was asked to come to Missouri where he would be ordained an apostle. Before he could return, however, the Saints were driven from the state by Gov. Lilburn W. Boggs's extermination order. Elder Woodruff spent the winter in Illinois, then journeyed with Brigham Young and others to Far West, Missouri, where they had been appointed by revelation to depart on an overseas mission. While standing at the site of the Far West Temple, Wilford Woodruff was ordained an apostle by Brigham Young on April 26, 1839, and immediately left on a mission to England.

Elder Woodruff was one of the most effective missionaries to ever serve in Great Britain. Shortly after his arrival there, he was directed by the voice of God to travel to Herefordshire. He found a group of over six hundred people who had left the Wesleyan Methodist faith. They called themselves the United Brethren and were searching intently for light and truth. "During the first thirty days after Wilford's arrival he baptized thirty-five preachers and one hundred sixty members of the United Brethren. Wilford was given the use of one chapel and fifty-four houses, allowing him to preach according to the law. This opened the door, and over eighteen hundred souls were baptized. Only one of the United Brethren failed to embrace the Gospel"

("Sacrifice Brings Forth the Blessings of Heaven," 161–62)

He wrote this summary of his missionary experiences for the year 1840:

"I traveled 4,469 miles, held 230 meetings, established 53 places for preaching, and planted 47 churches and jointly organized them. These churches chiefly comprised the two conferences raised up in Herefordshire, consisting of about 1,500 Saints, 28 elders, 110 priests, 24 teachers and 10 deacons. The baptisms of the year were 336 persons under my own hand, and I assisted at the baptism of 86 others. I baptized 57 preachers. . . . I confirmed 420 members . . . blessed 120 children, and administered to 120 sick, by prayer. . . . I assisted in procuring £1,000 for the publication of 3,000 copies of the Hymn Book, 5,000 copies of the Book of Mormon, for the printing of the *Millennial Star,* and to assist 200 Saints to emigrate to Nauvoo. I wrote 200 letters, and received 112" (*Wilford Woodruff, His Life and Labors,* 134).

"Never have I spent a year with more interest than 1840. Never have I been called to make greater sacrifices or enjoyed greater blessings" (*Wilford Woodruff's Journal,* 1:586–87; December 31, 1840).

Elder Woodruff was a tireless and devoted missionary as has ever served. Following are several remarkable incidents he experienced as a missionary.

Desires to Serve As a Missionary

After Wilford Woodruff received the gospel, he felt an intense desire to deliver in turn the same message that had brought him such joy, such assurance, such satisfaction in the service of the Master. The message that came to him was the most glorious event of his life, and it is quite natural that he should wish to be a messenger of the same divine truth to others. The talents with which he had been endowed by his Maker awakened within him those hopes, aspirations, and ambitions that were in harmony with those gifts which were peculiar to the man. His talents made him preeminently a messenger of salvation to the world. It is no wonder that he was prompted by a heartfelt desire to bestow upon others that which had come with such joy and with such abundance to him.

He wanted to go on a mission but felt that he should be called, and yet he sincerely believed that the Lord would prompt those whose duty it was to bestow upon him such an honor, such a privilege. He retired to the woods in prayer. There upon his knees in humility and childlike simplicity, he told the Lord his wishes and his hopes. He asked Him, if it was within His holy will, that the way might be opened for him to preach the gospel in the world. "Before I arose from my knees," he says, "the spirit of the Lord rested upon me and bore witness that my prayer was heard and should be answered upon my head. I arose very happy and walked through thick woods about forty rods into an open road. As I entered the roadway, I met Judge Elias Higbee. Brother Hibgee was a high priest and a very faithful man, one of the noblest men of God in the last days. I had associated with him daily, but never mentioned to him my desire to preach the gospel. To my surprise, as soon as I approached him he said: 'Brother Wilford, the spirit of the Lord tells me that you should be ordained to go and preach the gospel.'"

A few days later, on November 5, 1834, by vote of the branch of the Church at Adam-ondi-Ahman, Wilford Woodruff was ordained a priest by Simeon Carter, who also ordained Stephen Winchester and Heman Hyde at the same meeting. He received his license and by appointment of Bishop Partridge was assigned to Arkansas and Tennessee. In eight days, he left to perform his mission, to be one of the very foremost in introducing the gospel into the Southern States—a section of the Union where, since then, so many thousands have received the gospel and have been gathered to Zion. His faith had been great. The spirit of the Lord rested upon him, and his prayers were promptly answered (*Wilford Woodruff, His Life and Labors,* 47).

First Mission: Arkansas and Tennessee (1834–1836)

The Ministering of Angels

While serving as president of the Church, Wilford Woodruff bore testimony of the ministration of angels he experienced while serving his first mission. He declared that he was never more blessed than as a priest in the Aaronic Priesthood while fulfilling a mission:

I had the administration of angels while holding the office of a priest. I had visions and revelations. I traveled thousands of miles. I baptized men, though I could not confirm them because I had not the authority to do it. (*The Discourses of Wilford Woodruff,* 298)

Travels without Purse or Scrip

The law of God to us in those days was to go without purse or scrip. Our journey lay through Jackson County, from which the Saints had just been driven, and it was dangerous for a Mormon to be found in that part of the state. We put some Books of Mormon and some clothing into our valises, strapped these on our backs, and started on foot. We crossed the ferry into Jackson County, and went through it. In some instances the Lord preserved us, as it were by miracle, from the mob. We dared not go to houses and get food, so we picked and ate raw corn, slept on the ground, and did any way we could until we got out of the county. . . .

In the southern part of Missouri and the northern part of Arkansas, in 1834, there were very few inhabitants. We visited a place called Harmony Mission, on the Osage River, one of the most crooked rivers in the West. This mission was kept by a Presbyterian minister and his family. We arrived there on Sunday night at sunset. We had walked all day without anything to eat, and were very hungry and tired. Neither the minister nor his wife would give us anything to eat, or let us stay over night, because we were Mormons, and the only chance we had was to go twelve miles farther down the river, to an Osage Indian trading post kept by a Frenchman named Jereu; and the wicked priest who would not give us a piece of bread lied to us about the road, and sent us across the swamp, where we wallowed knee-deep in mud and water till ten o'clock at night, in trying to follow the crooked river. We then left the swamp and put out into the prairie, to lie in the grass for the night.

When we got out of the swamp, we heard an Indian drumming on a tin pail and singing. It was very dark, but we traveled toward the noise, and when we drew near the Indian camp quite a number of large Indian dogs came out to meet us. They smelled us, but did not bark or bite. Soon we were surrounded by Osage Indians, and were kindly received by Mr. Jereu and his wife who was an Indian. She gave us an excellent supper and a good bed, which we were thankful for after the fatigue of the day.

As I laid my head upon my pillow, I felt to thank God from the bottom of my heart for the exchange from the barbarous treatment of a civilized Presbyterian priest to the humane, kind, and generous treatment of the savage Osage Indians. May God reward them both according to their deserts! (*Wilford Woodruff, His Life and His Labors*, 47–48)

Encounters Wild Animals

We arose in the morning, after a good night's rest. I was somewhat lame, from wading in the swamp the night before. We had a good breakfast. Mr. Jereu sent an Indian to see us across the river, and informed us that it was sixty miles to the nearest settlement of either white or red men.

We were too bashful to ask for anything to take with us to eat; so we crossed the river and started on our day's journey of sixty miles without a morsel of food of any kind. We started about sunrise and crossed a thirty-mile prairie, apparently as level as a house floor, without shrub or water. We arrived at timber about two o'clock in the afternoon.

As we approached the timber, a large black bear came out towards us. We were not afraid of him, for we were on the Lord's business, and had not mocked God's prophets as did the forty-two wicked children who said to Elisha, "Go up thou bald head," for which they were torn by bears. When the bear got within eight rods of us he sat on his haunches, looked at us a moment, and ran away; and we went on our way rejoicing.

We had to travel in the night, which was cloudy and very dark, so we had great difficulty to keep the road. Soon a large drove of wolves gathered around, and followed us. They came very close, and at times it seemed as though they would eat us up. We had materials for striking a light, and at ten o'clock, not knowing where we were, and the wolves becoming so bold. We thought it wisdom to make a fire; so we stopped and gathered a lot of oak limbs that lay on the ground, and lit them, and as our fire began to burn the wolves left us.

As we were about to lay down on the ground—for we had no blankets—we heard a dog bark. My companion said it was a wolf; I said it was a dog; but soon we heard a cowbell. Then we each took a firebrand, went about a quarter of a mile, and found the house, which was sixty miles from where we started that morning. It was an old log cabin, about twelve feet square, with no door, but an old blanket was hung up in the doorway. There was no furniture except one bedstead, upon which lay a woman, several children, and several small dogs.

A man lay on the bare floor with his feet to the fireplace, and all were asleep. I went in and spoke to the man, but did not wake him. I stepped up to him, and laid my hand on his shoulder. The moment he felt the weight of my hand he jumped to his feet and ran around the room as though he were frightened; but he was quieted when we informed him we were friends. The cause of his fright was that he had shot a panther a few nights before, and he thought its mate had jumped upon him. He asked us what we wanted; we told him we wished to stop with him all night, and would like something to eat. He informed us we might lie on the floor as he did, but that he had not a mouthful for us to eat, as he had to depend on his gun to get breakfast for his family in the morning. So we lay on the bare floor, and slept through a long, rainy night, which was pretty hard after walking sixty miles without anything to eat. That was the hardest day's work of my life. The man's name was Williams. He was in the mob in Jackson County; and after the Saints were driven out, he, with many others, went south. (*Wilford Woodruff, His Life and Labors,* 48–50)

Missouri Hospitality

We got up in the morning and walked in the rain twelve miles to the house of a man named Bemon, who was also one of the mob from Jackson County. The family were about to sit down to breakfast as we came in. In those days it was the custom of the Missourians to ask you to eat even though they were hostile to you;

so he asked us to take breakfast, and we were very glad of the invitation. He knew we were Mormons; and as soon as we began to eat, he began to swear about the Mormons. He had a large platter of bacon and eggs, and plenty of bread on the table, and his swearing did not hinder our eating, for the harder he swore the harder we ate, until we got our stomachs full; then we arose from the table, took our hats, and thanked him for our breakfast. The last we heard of him he was still swearing. I trust the Lord will reward him for our breakfast. (*Wilford Woodruff, His Life and Labors,* 50)

Strange Encounter with the Akeman Family
(In some accounts, this name appears as Hakeman)

In the early days of the Church, it was a great treat to an elder in his travels through the country to find a Mormon; it was so with us. We were hardly in Arkansas when we heard of a family named Akeman. They were in Jackson County in the persecutions. Some of the sons had been tied up there and whipped on their bare backs, with hickory switches, by the mob. We heard of their living on Petit Jean River, in the Arkansas Territory, and we went a long way to visit them. . . .

We arrived that night within five miles of Mr. Akeman's, and were kindly entertained by a stranger. During the night I had the following dream: I thought an angel came to us, and told us we were commanded of the Lord to follow a certain straight path, which was pointed out to us, let it lead us wherever it might. After we had walked in it awhile we came to the door of a house, which was in the line of a high wall running north and south, so that we could not go around. I opened the door and saw the room was filled with large serpents, and I shuddered at the sight. My companion said he would not go into the room for fear of the serpents. I told him I would try to go through the room though they [would kill] me, for the Lord commanded it. As I stepped into the room the serpents coiled themselves up, and raised their heads some two feet from the floor, to spring at me. There was one much larger than the rest, in the center of the room, which raised his head nearly as high as mine and made a spring at me. At that instant I felt as though nothing but the power of God could save me, and I stood still. Just before the serpent reached me he dropped dead at my feet; all the rest dropped dead, swelled up, turned black, bust open, took fire and were consumed before my eyes, and we went through the room unharmed, thanking God for our deliverance.

I awoke in the morning and pondered upon the dream. We took breakfast, and started on our journey on Sunday morning to visit Mr. Akeman. I related to my companion my dream, and told him we should see something strange. We had great anticipations of meeting Mr. Akeman, supposing him to be a member of the Church. When we arrived at his house, he received us very coldly, and we soon found that he had apostatized. He brought railing accusations against the Book of Mormon and the authorities of the Church.

Word was sent through all the settlements on the river for twenty miles that two Mormon preachers were in the place. A mob was soon raised, and warning sent to us to leave immediately or we would be tarred and feathered, ridden on a rail, and hanged. I soon saw who the serpents were. My companion wanted to leave; I told him, no. I would stay and see my dream fulfilled.

There was an old gentleman and lady named Hubbel, who had read the Book of Mormon and believed. Father Hubbel came to see us, and invited us to make our home with him while we stayed in the place. We did so, and labored for him some three weeks with our axes, clearing land, while we were waiting to see the salvation of God.

February 14th, 1835, was an important day to me. In company with Brother Brown, I took my axe [and] went into the woods to help Brother Hubbel clear some land. We chopped till 3 o'clock in the afternoon. The spirit of the Lord came upon me like a rushing of mighty wind. The voice of the spirit said, "Go up again and visit Mr. Akeman and again bear testimony to him of the truth of the Book of Mormon and of the work of God." I marveled at this and told Brother Brown what the spirit said to me. He replied that I might go if I wished to do so, but that he would not go. I carried my ax to the house and walked up to Mr. Akeman's about one and a half miles through a pleasant grove. While on my way I reflected upon this strange operation of the spirit within me. I was in a deep, gloomy frame of mind and thought. As I approached the house I saw the door open and Mr. Akeman walking the floor. I felt particularly impressed to ask if he was well. He said he never felt better in health. I told him I had come to bear testimony again to him of the truth of the Book of Mormon and of the work of God and of the danger of opposing that work. He was soon filled with wrath and indignation and he opposed me in the strongest terms and raged against the leaders of the Church. My mouth was more closed up than ever before. I felt that the house was filled with devils and with an awful darkness. I felt horrible. I did not understand why the Lord should send me into the midst of such spirits to bear testimony of his work. I felt very strange. My tongue seemed glued to my mouth. I could not speak. I arose to my feet to leave the house. I felt as though the floor moved under my feet and when I stepped upon the ground I felt as though I was surrounded by evil spirits. I had a desire to flee as Lot did when he went out of Sodom, without looking behind me. Mr. Akeman followed me out of the door and kept within about four rods of me. Neither of us spoke a word. I knew he was following, but when he was about four rods from the house, the strange feeling left me. When Mr. Akeman reached the place where my feelings so instantly changed, he fell dead at my feet as though he had been struck with a thunderbolt from heaven. I heard him fall to the earth, but I did not look behind me. His daughter stood in the doorway and saw him fall. She fainted and fell at about the same time. Neither of them spoke a word that I could hear. I continued to walk down to Mr. Hubbel's as fast as I could, meditating all the while upon the strange dealings of God with me. I still did not know that Mr. Akeman was dead. I arrived at Mr. Hubbel's just at dark in a peculiar state of mind. Supper was ready. We all sat down to the table. The blessing was asked, and I took up my knife and fork and began to eat, when I heard a horse coming up on the full ran. I dropped my knife and fork and listened. A man rode up to our door and cried out: "Mr. Akeman is dead. I want you to go there immediately." In a moment my eyes were opened, so that I understood the whole matter. I felt satisfied with the dealings of God with me in calling me to go and warn him. As soon as his daughter, who fell to the ground about the same time, came to her senses, she ran to her nearest brother and gave the alarm.

We walked up to Mr. Akeman's house as soon as we could. When we arrived there, we found all his sons in the house around his body wailing in an awful manner. He was naturally a large man, but his body was swollen to a great extent. It appeared as though his skin were ready to burst open. He was black as an African. We at once went to work and made a large box in which to put him. I continued to think of my dream, which I had had some time before the events here related took place.

His family, as well as ourselves, felt it was the judgment of God upon him. I preached his funeral sermon. Many of the mob died suddenly. We stayed about two weeks after Akeman's death and preached, baptized Mr. Hubbel and his wife, and then continued on our journey. (*Wilford Woodruff, His Life and Labors,* 50–54)

A Good Night's Rest

We concluded to go down the Arkansas River and cross into Tennessee. We could not get passage on the boat, because of the low water; so we went on the bank of the river and cut down a sound cottonwood tree, three feet through, and cut off a twelve foot length from the butt end; in two days we dug out a canoe. We made a pair of oars and a rudder, and on the 11th day of March, 1835, we launched our canoe, and commenced our voyage down the Arkansas River, without provisions.

The first day we sailed twenty-five miles, and stopped at night with a poor family who lived on the bank of the river. These kind folks gave us supper and breakfast, and, in the morning, gave us johnny-cake and a piece of pork to take with us on our journey. We traveled about fifty miles that day, and at night stopped at an old tavern, in a village called Cadron, which was deserted because it was believed to be haunted by evil spirits. We made a fire in the tavern, roasted a piece of our pork, ate our supper, said our prayers, went into a chamber, lay down on the bare floor, and were soon asleep. I dreamed I was at my father's house in a good feather bed, and I had a good night's rest. When I awoke the bed vanished, and I found myself on the bare floor and well rested, not having been troubled with evil spirits or anything else. (*Wilford Woodruff, His Life and Labors,* 54)

Abandoned by His Companion

On the 24th of March, after traveling some ten miles through mud, I was made lame with a sharp pain in my knee, and sat down on a log. My companion, who was anxious to get to his home in Kirtland, left me sitting in an alligator swamp. I did not see him again for two years. I knelt down in the mud and prayed, and the Lord healed me and I went on my way rejoicing. (*Wilford Woodruff, His Life and Labors,* 54–55)

"I Did Not Look Much Like a Preacher"

On the 27th of March I arrived at Memphis, weary and hungry. I went to the best tavern in the place, kept by Mr. Josiah Jackson. I told him I was a stranger and had no money, and asked him if he would keep me over night. He inquired what my business was, and I told him I was a preacher of the gospel. He laughed and said that I did not look much like a preacher. I did not blame him, as most of the preachers he ever had been acquainted with rode on fine horses or in fine carriages, dressed in broadcloth, had large salaries, and would likely see this whole world sink to perdition before they would wade through one hundred and seventy miles of mud to save the people.

The landlord wanted a little fun, so said he would keep me if I would preach. He wanted to see if I could preach. I must confess that by this time I became a little mischievous, and pleaded with him not to set me preaching. The more I pleaded to be excused the more determined Mr. Jackson was that I should preach. He took my valise, and the landlady got me a good supper. I sat down in a large hall to eat. Before I got through, the room began to be filled by some of the rich and fashionable people of Memphis, dressed in their broadcloth and silk, while my appearance was such as you can imagine, after traveling through the mud as I had done. When I had finished eating, the table was carried out of the room over the heads of the people. I was placed in the corner of the room, with a stand having a Bible, hymn book, and candle on it, hemmed in by a dozen men, with the landlord in the center.

There were present some five hundreds persons, who had come together, not to hear a gospel sermon, but to have some fun. I read a hymn, and asked them to sing. Not a soul would sing a word. I told them I had not the gift of singing; but with the help of the Lord, I would both pray and preach. I knelt down to pray, and the men around me dropped on their knees. I prayed to the Lord to give me His spirit and to show me the hearts of the people. I promised the Lord, in my prayer, that I would deliver to that congregation whatever He would give to me. I arose and spoke one hour and a half, and it was one of the best sermons of my life. The lives of the congregation were open to the vision of my mind, and I told them of their wicked deeds and the reward they would obtain. The men who surrounded me dropped their heads. Three minutes after I closed, I was the only person in the room.

Soon I was shown to a bed, in a room adjoining a large one in which were assembled many of the men whom I had been preaching to. I could hear their conversation. One man said he would like to know how that Mormon boy knew of their past lives. In a little while they got to disputing about some doctrinal point. One suggested calling me to decide the point. The landlord said, "No; we have had enough for once." In the morning, I had a good breakfast. The landlord said if I came that way again to stop at his house, and stay as long as I might choose. (*Wilford Woodruff, His Life and Labors,* 55–56)

"A Bright Light Shone around Us"

On the following day [October 21, 1835] I preached at the house of Benjamin L. Clapp, and baptized seven Campbellites and one Baptist. On the 16th of November, I preached at Brother Camp's, and baptized three. On the day following, it being Sunday, I preached again at Brother Clapp's, and baptized five.

At the close of the meeting I mounted my horse to ride to Clark's River, in company with Seth Utley, four other brethren, and two sisters. The distance was twenty miles. We came to a stream which was so swollen by rains that we could not cross without swimming our horses. To swim would not be safe for the women, so we went up the stream to find a ford. In the attempt we were overtaken by a severe storm of wind and rain, lost our way in the darkness, and wandered through creeks and mud. But the Lord does not forsake His Saints in any of their troubles. While we were in the woods suffering under the blast of the storm, groping like the blind for the wall, a bright light suddenly shone around us, and revealed to us our dangerous situation on the edge of a gulf. The light continued with us until we found the road; we then went on our way rejoicing, though the darkness returned and the rain continued. We reached Brother Henry Thomas' in safety about nine o'clock at night, having been five hours in the storm, and forded streams many times. None of us felt to complain, but were thankful to God for His preserving care. On the following day I preached at Damon Creek, and organized a branch called Damon Creek Branch, and ordained Daniel Thomas a teacher. (*Wilford*

Woodruff, His Life and Labors, 57–58)

Summary of 1835 Mission Experiences

This brings the year 1835 to a close—the first year of my mission—during which time I had traveled three thousand two hundred and forty-eight miles, held one hundred and seventy meetings, baptized forty-three persons—three of whom were Campbellite preachers—assisted Elder Parrish to baptize twenty more, confirmed thirty-five, organized three branches, ordained two teachers and one deacon, procured thirty subscribers for the Messenger and Advocate, one hundred and seventy-three signers to the petition to the governor of Missouri for redress of wrongs done the Saints in Jackson County, had three mobs rise against me—but was not harmed—wrote eighteen letters, received ten, and, finally, closed the labors of the year 1835 by eating johnny cake, butter and honey, at Brother A. O. Smoot's. (*Wilford Woodruff, His Life and Labors,* 58)

Called to Second Quorum of the Seventy

I spent the fore part of January, 1836, (the weather being very cold), at the house of A. O. Smoot, in Kentucky, studying Kirkham's English Grammar. I continued to travel and preach in Kentucky and Tennessee and baptized all that would believe my testimony. On the 26th of February we held a conference at the house of Brother Lewis Clapp (father of B. L. Clapp). There were represented one hundred and three members in that mission. I ordained A. O. Smoot and Benjamin Boyston elders, and Daniel Thomas and Benjamin

L. Clapp priests. I also ordained one teacher and two deacons.

After conference I took Brothers Smoot and Clapp with me to preach. The former traveled with me constantly till the 21st of April, when we had the privilege of meeting with Elder David W. Patten, who had come direct from Kirtland, and who had been ordained one of the Twelve Apostles. It was a happy meeting. He gave us an account of the endowments at Kirtland, the glorious blessings received, the ministration of angels, the organization of the Twelve Apostles and seventies, and informed me that I was appointed a member of the second quorum of seventy. All this was glorious news to me, and caused my heart to rejoice. On the 27th of May we were joined by Elder Warren Parrish, direct from Kirtland. We had a happy time together. (*Wilford Woodruff, His Life and Labors*, 58–59)

"Trial by a Mob Court"

A warrant was issued, on the oath of a priest, against D. W. Patten, W. Parrish and myself. We were accused in the warrant of the great "crime" of testifying that Christ would come in this generation, and that we promised the Holy Ghost to those whom we baptized. Brothers Patten and Parrish were taken on the 19th of June. I, being in another county, escaped arrest. The brethren were put under two thousand dollars bonds to appear at court. Albert Petty and Seth Utley were their bondsmen. They were tried on the 22nd of June. They pleaded their own cause. Although men came forward and testified that they did receive the Holy Ghost after they were baptized, the brethren were condemned; but finally were released by paying the expenses of the mob court.

One peculiar circumstance was connected with this trial by a mob court, which was armed to the teeth. When the trial was through, the people were not willing to permit more than one to speak. Warren Parrish had said a few words, and they were not willing to let David Patten say anything; but he, feeling the injustice of the court, and being filled with the power of God, arose to his feet and delivered a speech of about twenty minutes, holding them spell-bound while he told them of their wickedness and of the abominations they were guilty of, also of the curse of God that awaited them, if they did not repent, and for taking up two harmless, inoffensive men for preaching the gospel of Christ. When he had got through his speech the judge said, "You must be armed with secret weapons, or you would not talk in this fearless manner to an armed court." Brother Patten replied, "I have weapons that you know not of, and they are given me of God, for He gives me all the power I have." The judge seemed willing to get rid of them upon almost any terms, and offered to dismiss them if their friends would pay the costs, which the brethren present freely offered to do.

When the two were released, they mounted their horses and rode a mile to Seth Utley's; but as soon as they had left, the court became ashamed that they had been let go so easily, and the whole mob mounted their horses to follow them to Utley's. One of the Saints, seeing the state of affairs, went on before the mob to notify the brethren, so that they had time to ride into the woods near by. They traveled along about three miles to Brother Albert Petty's, and went to bed. The night was dark, and they fell asleep, but Brother Patten was warned in a dream to get up and flee, as the mob soon would be there. They both arose, saddled their animals, and rode into the adjoining county. The house they had just left was soon surrounded by the mob, but the brethren escaped through the mercy of God. (*Wilford Woodruff, His Life and Labors*, 59–60)

Willingness to Preach Anywhere

I was invited to hold a meeting at a Baptist meetinghouse; this was on the 27th of June. On my arrival I met a large congregation, but, on commencing services, Parson Browning ordered the meeting to be closed. I told the people I had come ten miles to preach the gospel to them, and was willing to stand in a cart, on a pile of wood, on a fence, or any other place they would appoint, to have that privilege. One man said he owned the fence and land in front of the meetinghouse, and we might use both, for he did not believe Mormonism would hurt either. So the congregation crossed the road, took down the fence and made seats of it, and I preached to them one hour and a half.

At the close, Mr. Randoph Alexander bore testimony to the truth of what had been said. He invited me home with him, bought a Book of Mormon and was baptized, and I organized a branch in that place. (*Wilford Woodruff, His Life and Labors*, 60–61)

Horse Poisoned by a Mob

On Sunday, the 31st of July, A. O. Smoot and I preached at Mr. David Crider's, Weakley County, Tennessee. After the meeting, Mr. Crider was baptized. A mob gathered and threatened us, and poisoned our horses, so that the one I rode, belonging to Samuel West, died a few days after. This horse had carried me thousands of miles while preaching the gospel. (*Wilford Woodruff, His Life and Labors*, 61)

Second Mission: Eastern States and Fox Islands (1837–1838)

Opposition While Preaching in Fox Islands

Mr. Newton, the Baptist minister, now commenced a war against us, and sent to the South Island for a Mr. Douglass, a Methodist minister, with whom he had been at variance for years, to come over and help him put down "Mormonism." Mr. Douglass came over and they got together as many people as they could, and held a conference. He railed against Joseph, the Prophet, and the Book of Mormon, and taking that book in his hand, with outstretched arm, declared that he feared none of the judgments of God that would come upon him for rejecting it as the word of God. . . .

When he closed I arose and informed the people that I would meet them the next Sunday in the meetinghouse and answer Mr. Douglass; and I wished him, as well as the people, to be present. I informed the people that Mr. Douglass had made many false statements against Joseph Smith and the Latter-day Saints, with whom he had no acquaintance; and he had misquoted much Scripture, all of which I would correct.

We continued to baptize the people on North Island until we baptized every person who owned an interest in the Baptist meeting-house. I then followed Mr. Douglass home to South Island, and preached the gospel to the members of his church, and baptized nearly all of them.

The excitement became great on both islands, and on Sunday, the 17th of September, I met a large assembly from both islands, and took up the same subject that Mr. Douglass had dwelt upon in his remarks against the Book of Mormon and our principles. I spoke two and a half hours, and answered every objection against the Book of Mormon, Joseph Smith, or our principles. I had good attention, and the people seemed satisfied. At the close of the meeting Elder Hale administered the ordinance of baptism. (*Leaves from My Journal*, 34–35)

Third and Fourth Missions: England (1839–1841, 1844–1846)

Sacrifices Made to Serve

In August 1839, Elder Woodruff left his home to join a number of other missionaries and members of the Twelve in Liverpool, England. This mission required additional sacrifice as Elder Woodruff was required to leave his wife suffering of very ill health, making his departure particularly heartrending.

Early upon the morning of the 8th of August, 1839, I arose from my bed of sickness, laid my hands upon the head of my sick wife, Phoebe, and blessed her. I then departed from the embrace of my companion, and left her almost without food or the necessaries of life.

She parted from me with the fortitude that becomes a Saint, realizing the responsibilities of her companion. I quote from my journal: "Phoebe, farewell! Be of good cheer; remember me in your prayers. I leave these pages for your perusal when I am gone. I shall see thy face again in the flesh. I go to obey the commands of Jesus Christ."

Although feeble, I walked to the banks of the Mississippi River. There President Brigham Young took me in a canoe (having no other conveyance) and paddled me across the river.

When we landed, I lay down on a side of sole leather, by the post office, to rest.

Brother Joseph, the Prophet of God, came along and looked at me.

"Well, Brother Woodruff," said he, "you have started upon your mission."

"Yes," said I, "but I feel and look more like a subject for the dissecting room than a missionary."

Joseph replied: "What did you say that for? Get up, and go along; all will be right with you!" (*Leaves from My Journal*, 69)

Generosity of the Apostles

As they started on their mission, Elders John Taylor and Wilford Woodruff passed Elder Parley P. Pratt who was hewing a log, preparatory to building a cabin for his family. Elder Pratt said, "Brother Woodruff, I have no money, but I have an empty purse, which I will give you." A few rods farther they met Elder Heber C. Kimball who was also hewing a log to build a cabin. Brother Kimball said, "As Parley has given you a purse, I have got a dollar I will give you to put in it" (Church History and Modern Revelation, 4:50).

Baptizes While Being Stoned by Mob

Opposition grew as the Church prospered in the area. While preaching in the village of Hawcross, Wilford Woodruff was surrounded by a hostile mob. When some of the villagers requested baptism, Wilford told them that if they had faith enough to be baptized, he had sufficient faith to administer the ordinance, in spite of the threatened physical violence. The small group walked down to a pond and was soon surrounded by a mob armed with stones. Wilford Woodruff reported, "I walked into the water with my mind stayed on God and baptized five persons while they were pelting my body with stones, one of which hit me on the head and came very near knocking me down" ("Elder Woodruff's Letter," Times and Seasons *2 (March 1, 1841): 330–31).*

Miraculous Conversions at the Benbow Farm

March 1st, 1840, was my birthday, when I was thirty-three years of age. It being Sunday, I preached twice through the day to a large assembly in the City Hall, in the town of Hanley, and administered the sacrament unto the Saints.

In the evening I again met with a large assembly of the Saints and strangers, and while singing the first hymn [I felt] the Spirit of the Lord resting upon me, and the voice of God said to me, "This is the last meeting that you will hold with this people for many days."

I was astonished at this, as I had many appointments out in that district.

When I arose to speak to the people, I told them that it was the last meeting I should hold with them for many days. They were as much astonished as I was.

At the close of the meeting four persons came forward for baptism, and we went down in to the water and baptized them.

In the morning I went in secret before the Lord, and asked him what his will was concerning me.

The answer I got was, that I should go to the south, for the Lord had a great work for me to perform there, as many souls were waiting for the word of the Lord.

On the 3rd of March, 1840, in fulfillment of the word of the Lord to me, I took coach and rode to Wolverhampton, twenty-six miles, and spent the day there.

On the morning of the 4th I again took coach, and rode through Dudley, Stourbridge, Stourport, and Worchester, and then walked a number of miles to Mr. John Benbow's, Hill Farm, Castle Frome, Ledbury, Herefordshire. This was a farming country in the south of England, a region where no elder of the Latter-day Saints had visited.

I found Mr. Benbow to be a wealthy farmer, cultivating three hundred acres of land, occupying a good mansion, and having plenty of means. His wife, Jane, had no children.

I presented myself to him as a missionary from America, an elder of the Church of Jesus Christ of Latter-day Saints, who had been sent to him by the commandment of God as a messenger of salvation, to preach the gospel of life unto him and his household, and the inhabitants of the land.

Mr. Benbow and his wife received me with glad hearts and thanksgiving. It was in the evening when I arrived, having traveled forty-eight miles by coach and on foot during the day, but after receiving refreshments we sat down together, and conversed until two o'clock in the morning.

Mr. Benbow and his wife rejoiced greatly at the glad tidings which I brought unto them of the fulness of the everlasting gospel, which God had revealed through the mouth of his Prophet, Joseph Smith, in these last days.

I rejoiced greatly at the news that Mr. Benbow gave me, that there was a company of men and women—over six hundred in number—who had broken off from the Wesleyan Methodist, and taken the name of United Brethren. They had forty-five preachers among them and had chapels and many houses that were licensed according to the law of the land for preaching in.

This body of United Brethren were searching for light and truth, but had gone as far as they could, and were continually calling upon the Lord to open the way before them, and send them light and knowledge that they might know the true way to be saved.

When I heard these things, I could clearly see why the Lord had commanded me, while in the town of Hanley, to leave that place of labor and go to the south, for in Herefordshire there was a great harvest-field for gathering many Saints into the kingdom of God.

I retired to my bed with joy after offering my prayers and thanksgiving to God, and slept sweetly until the rising of the sun.

I arose on the morning of the 5th, took breakfast, and told Mr. Benbow I would like to commence my Master's business, by preaching the gospel to the people.

He had a large hall in his mansion which was licensed for preaching, and he sent word through the neighborhood that an American missionary would preach at his house that evening.

As the time drew nigh many of the neighbors came in, and I preached my first gospel sermon in the house. I also preached on the following evening at the same place, and baptized six persons, including Mr. John Benbow and his wife, and four preachers of the United Brethren.

I spent most of the following day in clearing out a pool of water, and preparing it for baptizing in, as I saw many to be baptized there. I afterwards baptized six hundred in that pool of water. (*Wilford Woodruff, His Life and Labors,* 116–17)

Warrant Issued for Elder Woodruff's Arrest

On Sunday, the 8th, I preached at Frome's Hill in the morning, at Standley Hill in the afternoon, and at John

Benbow's Hill Farm in the evening.

The parish church that stood in the neighborhood of Brother Benbow's, presided over by the rector of the parish, was attended during the day by only fifteen persons, while I had a large congregation, estimated to number a thousand, attend my meeting through the day and evening.

When I arose in the evening to speak at Brother Benbow's house, a man entered the door and informed me that he was a constable, and had been sent by the rector of the parish with a warrant to arrest me.

I asked him, "For what crime?"

He said, "For preaching to the people."

I told him that I, as well as the rector, had a license for preaching the gospel to the people, and that if he would take a chair I would wait upon him after meeting.

He took my chair and sat beside me. I preached the first principles of the everlasting gospel for an hour and a quarter. The power of God rested upon me, the Spirit filled the house, and the people were convinced.

At the close of the meeting I opened a door for baptism, and seven offered themselves. Among the number were four preachers and the constable.

The latter arose and said, "Mr. Woodruff, I would like to be baptized."

I told him I would like to baptize him. I went down to the pool and baptized seven. We then met together, and I confirmed thirteen and broke bread unto the Saints, and we all rejoiced together.

The constable went to the rector and told him if he

wanted Mr. Woodruff taken up for preaching the gospel, he must go himself and serve the writ, for he had heard him preach the only true gospel sermon he had ever listened to in his life.

The rector did not know what to make of it, so he sent two clerks of the Church of England as spies, to attend our meeting, and find out what we did preach.

But they were both pricked in their hearts and received the word of the Lord gladly and were baptized and confirmed members of the Church of Jesus Christ of Latter-day Saints.

The rector became alarmed and did not dare to send anybody else. (*Leaves from My Journal*, 80–81)

Baptizes More Than Two Hundred People

The ministers and rectors of the south of England called a convention and sent a petition to the Archbishop of Canterbury, to request Parliament to pass a law prohibiting the "Mormons" from preaching in the British dominion. In this petition the rector stated that one "Mormon" missionary had baptized fifteen hundred persons, mostly members of the English church, during the last seven months.

But the archbishop and council, knowing well that the laws of England gave free toleration to all religions under the British flag, sent word to the petitioners that if they had the worth of souls at heart as much as they had the ground where hares, foxes, and hounds ran, they would not lose so many of their flock.

I continued to preach and baptize daily.

On the 21st day of March I baptized Elder Thomas

Kingston. He was the superintendent of both preachers and members of the United Brethren.

The first thirty days after my arrival in Herefordshire, I had baptized forty-five preachers and one hundred-and-sixty members of the United Brethren, who put into my hands one chapel and forty-five houses, which were licensed according to law to preach in.

This opened a wide field for labor and enabled me to bring into the Church, through the blessing of God, over eighteen hundred souls during eight months, including all of the six hundred United Brethren except one person; also including some two hundred preachers of various denominations. (*Leaves from My Journal*, 81)

Credits God with His Success

The power of God rested upon us and upon the mission.

The sick were healed, devils were cast out, and the lame were made to walk. . . .

The whole history of this Herefordshire mission shows the importance of listening to the still small voice of the Spirit of God and the revelations of the Holy Ghost.

The Lord had a people there prepared for the gospel. They were praying for light and truth, and the Lord sent me to them, and I declared the gospel of life and salvation unto them, and some eighteen hundred souls received it, and many of them have been gathered to Zion in these mountains. Many of them have also been called to officiate in the bishopric, and have done much good in Zion. But in all these things we should ever acknowledge the hand of God, and give him the honor, praise and glory, forever and ever. Amen. (*Leaves from My Journal*, 82–83)

The Prince of Darkness "Made War upon Me"

The prospect in London at that time was the darkest it had ever been in since entering the vineyard; but the Lord was with us, and we were not discouraged. On Sunday we met with the Saints three times at Brother Corner's, read the Book of Mormon, gave instruction, and broke bread unto them. We had a good time, although there were only about half a dozen present. I felt the Spirit bear testimony that there would be a work done in London.

Having retired to rest in good season, I fell asleep and slept until midnight, when I awoke and meditated upon the things of God until three o'clock in the morning. And, while forming a determination to warn the people in London, and by the assistance and inspiration of God to overcome the power of darkness, a person appeared to me whom I consider as the prince of darkness. He made war upon me and attempted to take my life. As he was about to overcome me I prayed to the Father, in the name of Jesus Christ, for help. I then had power over him and he left me, though I was much wounded. Afterwards three men dressed in white came to me and prayed with me, and I was healed immediately of all my wounds, and delivered of my troubles. (*Wilford Woodruff, His Life and Labors*, 130)

*"How many times have we been called by revelation to go to the right and left, here, there, and the other place, contrary to our expectation?" (*Discourses of Wilford Woodruff, *60). Wilford Woodruff spoke these words in describing some of the many experiences he had as a missionary. Because of his fearless obedience to the Spirit, no matter where it led, he had many great successes in the mission field.*

Chapter 5

Record Keeper Extraordinaire

Wilford Woodruff is likely the greatest record keeper the Church has ever known. He regarded his responsibility to keep a daily journal and record the words of prophets and apostles as a call from God. Because of his faithful record keeping, the Church has many of the discourses of early Church leaders that otherwise would have been lost with the passing away of those who heard them.

Dedication of the Church Historian's Office

An excerpt from the dedicatory prayer by Elder Wilford Woodruff, September 10, 1856, as recorded in his journal:

Wilt thou bless, O Lord, with thy holy spirit, this building, that we may never profane thy name in this house or dishonor the holy priesthood or bring approach upon thy cause or grieve thy holy spirit in any way. Bring to our remembrance all things necessary to be written in the history of the Church, and cause that papers and documents that are necessary may be brought to us that we may be enabled to compile a correct, useful, and proper history. (*Wilford Woodruff, His Life and Labors,* 371)

God's Servants Need to Write

I said there was one subject I wished to speak upon and that was writing and keeping a journal of the dealings of God with us. I have, many times, thought the Quorum of the Twelve and others considered me rather enthusiastic upon this subject; but when the Prophet Joseph organized the Quorum of the Twelve, he commanded them to write and keep a journal or history of their lives, and gave his reasons why they should do it. I think the Twelve Apostles and all the elders of Israel who bear the Holy Priesthood should keep a journal of their official acts and the dealings of God with them. I would be glad to read the acts of my forefathers if they had never heard of a God, but especially when men are called to stand at the head of a great dispensation like this, and to build up the kingdom of God on the earth to remain forever. They, of all men on earth, ought to write and keep a true and correct history of the rise and progress of that kingdom, of the revelations of Jesus Christ and His dealings with us as we travel along in our pilgrimage. (*Wilford Woodruff's Journal*, 7:54; January 20, 1872)

"I Have Always Felt It My Duty to Write"

I have had this spirit upon me since I first entered this Church. I was baptized [after] the first sermon I heard and from that day until now, I have kept a daily journal. Whenever I have heard Joseph Smith preach, teach, or prophesy, I have always felt it my duty to write it. I have always felt uneasy. I could not eat, drink, or sleep in peace until I did write it; and my mind has been so exercised upon this subject that when I heard Joseph Smith teach and I had not pencil and paper, I would go home and set down and write that whole sermon, almost word for word and sentence by sentence as it was delivered, and when I had written it, it was taken from me. I remembered it no more. (*Wilford Woodruff's Journal*, 7:55; January 20, 1872)

The Devil Opposes Record Keeping

[A knowledge of the importance of record keeping] was the gift of God to me and the question has often rested [upon] me, Why are these things so? Why has this subject rested upon me more than other men? Again another question has rested upon my mind many times. Why has the devil sought to take my life from the day I was born until now, more than other men? For I seem [to have been] a marked victim for the devil from the day I was born until now, and I can find but one answer, and that is the devil knew if I got into the Church of Jesus Christ of Latter-day Saints I would write the history of the Church and leave on record the doings, works, and teachings of the prophets and apostles, elders and saints in the latter days, and that I would attend to the ordinances of the House of God for my father's household and friends, both for the living and the dead. That preserving power has followed me all the way through my life. It has been with me upon my missions abroad as well as at home. It has followed me until the present day. (*Wilford Woodruff's Journal*, 7:55; January 20, 1872)

A Love for the Words of God

I have recorded nearly all the sermons and teachings that I ever heard Joseph Smith deliver and many of the Quorum of the Twelve. I have in my journals scores of sermons of President Brigham Young, that he does not know . . . exist on earth. So of Orson Hyde, Parley Pratt, Orson Pratt, and others. (*Wilford Woodruff's Journal*, 7:55–56; January 20, 1872)

"I Would There Were Ten"

One reason I have been moved upon to write in early days was [that] nearly all the historians appointed in the early history of the Church apostatized and took the journals away with them, which, in a measure, were lost to the Church. I still keep a daily journal, but I have not reported sermons much for many years, for we have had scribes and reporters to keep a record of the sayings of the prophets and apostles; and I rejoice and thank God, for it does my soul good to look upon these little boys, sons of Brother George Q. Cannon and others, set at the reporter's table and report the sermons as they are delivered from the mouths of the prophets and apostles. I would there were ten where there is but one. (*Wilford Woodruff's Journal*, 7:55–56; January 20, 1872)

Keeps Daily Journal for Thirty-Five Years

I have lived to see fifty-six new years, and I have kept a daily journal of my life for the last thirty-five years. In some measure, it has also been the life of others. (*The Presidents of the Church*, 125)

"Should the Knowledge of These Things Slumber?"

In 1849, Elder Orson Pratt expounded on the importance of keeping a journal and witness of God's goodness. While speaking to the members of the British Mission, he said, "If every elder had, during the last nineteen years, kept a faithful record of all that he had seen, heard, and felt of the goodness, wisdom and power of God, the Church would now have been in possession of many thousand volumes, containing much important and useful information. How many thousands have been miraculously healed in this Church, and yet no one has recorded the circumstances. Is this right? Should these miraculous manifestations of the power of God be forgotten and pass into oblivion? Should the knowledge of these things slumber in the hearts of those who witnessed them, and extend no further than their own verbal reports will carry them? . . . We should keep a record because Jesus has commanded it. We should keep a record because the same will benefit us and the generations of our *children after us. We should keep a record because it will furnish many important items for the general history of the Church, which would otherwise be lost" (*Millennial Star, *11:152).*

Recording the Miracles We See

We are not apt to think of the importance of events as they transpire with us, but we feel the importance of them afterwards. We are living in one of the most important generations that man ever lived [in] on earth, and we should write an account of those important transactions which are taking place before our eyes in fulfillment of the prophecies and the revelations of God. There is a great flood of revelations fulfilling in our day, and as they are transpiring before our eyes, we want a record made of them. (*Wilford Woodruff's Journal,* 4:444; September 6, 1856)

Record Keeping Is a Service to Mankind

I have never spent any of my time more profitably for the benefit of mankind than in my journal writing. . . . Some of the most glorious gospel sermons, truths, and revelations that were given from God to this people through the mouth of the Prophets Joseph, Brigham, Heber, and the Twelve could not be found upon the earth on record, only in my journals, and they are compiled in the Church history and transmitted to the Saints of God in all future generations. Does not this pay me for my trouble? It does. (*Wilford Woodruff's Journal,* 5:37; March 17, 1857)

A Testimony and Warning

God has inspired me to keep a journal and history of this Church, and I warn the future historians to give credence to my history of this Church and kingdom, for my testimony is true, and the truth of its record will be manifest in the world to come. (*Wilford Woodruff's Journal,* 7:359; July 5, 1877)

It is interesting to note that much of the seven volume History of the Church *was compiled from Wilford Woodruff's journals and writings. The Church owes an immense debt of gratitude to this faithful record keeper. President Woodruff's writings consist of nineteen journal volumes and more than seven thousand pages, and they span sixty-two years.* (Presidents of the Church, *65)*

Chapter 6

Tireless Temple Worker

Wilford Woodruff served as the first president of the St. George Temple, which was dedicated in 1877. He was later instrumental in organizing the Genealogical Society of Utah, to help gather and preserve family histories so that vicarious ordinances for deceased loved ones could be performed in temples.

Labors to Help Redeem the Dead

I spent this day in the Endowment House [in Salt Lake City]. Brother Samuel H. B. Smith baptized this day persons 1,207 times for the dead, the most ever baptized in this last dispensation in one day by one man, and probably the most ever baptized since the world began in one day by one man. Daniel H. Wells sealed for the dead 102 couple[s] and Wilford Woodruff 108 couple[s], total 210 sealings. (*Wilford Woodruff's Journal,* 7:287; October 11, 1876)

Dedication of the St. George Temple

The St. George Temple is the first temple in this dispensation where endowments and sealings for deceased loved ones were performed. President Woodruff noted:

This is a very important day to the Church and kingdom of God on the earth. President Brigham Young, the Apostles, Wilford Woodruff, Erastus Snow, and Brigham Young Jr., with some two thousand Saints, assembled within the walls of the temple of our God, built in St George, for the purpose of dedicating certain portions of it unto God, that we might be prepared to commence giving endowments and blessings and sealings unto the Saints. (*Wilford Woodruff's Journal,* 7:303; January 1, 1877)

President Woodruff recorded the sermon delivered by President Brigham Young on that sacred occasion:

At the Close of the prayer we returned to the Lower Court, when Elder Snow and Woodruff made a few remarks pertaining to the workings in the temple calling upon all who desired to come forth and attend to the ordinances for themselves and their dead. After which, President Brigham Young, had been so lame through the day with rheumatism in his feet [that he] had been carried through the house in a chair, by three men. But upon this occasion, he arose and walked into the lower stand and made the following remarks:

"I cannot consent in my feelings to retire from this house without exercising my strength, the strength of my lungs, stomach, and speaking organs in speaking to this people. I hardly dare to say what is in my heart to say to this people. Perhaps it will not be prudent but I will say a few encouraging things to the Latter-day Saints. That is, they ought to be encouraging.

"We that are here are enjoying a privilege that we have no knowledge of any other people enjoying since the days of Adam. Brethren and Sisters, do you understand this? It seems a great many of the people know nothing about it. It is true that Solomon built a temple for the purpose of giving endowments but from what we can learn of the history of that time, they gave very few if any endowments; and one of the High Priest was murdered by wicked and corrupt men, who had already begun to apostatize, because he would not reveal those things appertaining to the priesthood that [were] forbidden for him to reveal until he came to the proper place.

"I will not say but what Enoch had temples and officiated in them, but we have no account of it. We know that he raised up a people so pure and holy that they were not permitted to remain with the wicked inhabitants of the earth, but were taken to another place.

"We as Latter-day Saints have been laboring for over forty years, and the revelations given us in the first were to establish the kingdom by gathering the Saints, building temples, and organizing the people as the family of heaven here on the earth. We reared up a temple in Kirtland, but we had no basement in it, nor a font, or preparations to give endowments for the living or the dead. It was left by the Saints, [as] they [were] going to Missouri.

"Joseph located the site for the temple in Jackson County, Missouri, and pointed out the southeast corner of the temple in the year eighteen hundred thirty-one. [He] also laid the corner stone for a temple in Far West, Caldwell County, Missouri. But these temples were not built. We built one in Nauvoo. I could pick out several before me now that were there when it was built, and know just how much was finished and what was done. It is true we left Brethren there with instructions to finish it, and they got it nearly completed before it was burned, but the Saints did not enjoy it.

"Now we have a Temple which will all be finished in a few days, and of which there is enough completed to commence work therein, which has not been done since the days of Adam that we have any knowledge of. Now those that can see the spiritual atmosphere can see that many of the Saints are still glued to this earth, and lusting and longing after the thing of this world, in which there is no profit.

"It is true we should look after the things of this world and devote all to the building up of the kingdom of God. According to the present feeling of many of our brethren, they would arrogate to themselves this world and all that pertains to it, and cease not day nor night to see that it was devoted to the building up of the kingdom of the devil. And if they had the power, they would build a railroad to carry it to hell and establish themselves there. Where are the eyes and hearts of this people? Where is their interest for their own salvation and that of their forefathers? We enjoy privileges that are enjoyed by no one else on the face of the earth. Supposing we were awake to this thing, namely, the salvation of the human family, this house would be crowded as we hope it will be from Monday morning until Saturday night.

"This House was built here in this place purposely where it is warm and pleasant in the winter time, and comfortable to work also for the Lamanites and all those coming from the South, to receive their endowments and other blessings.

"What do you suppose the fathers would say if they could speak from the dead? Would they not say we 'have lain here thousand of years, here in this prison house, waiting for this dispensation to come. Here we are bound and fettered in the association of those who are filthy.' What would they whisper in our ears? Why, if they had the power, the very thunders of heaven would be in our ears if we could but realize the importance of the work we are engaged in. All the angels in heaven are looking at this little handful of people. So also are the devils in hell looking at this people too and trying to overthrow us; and the people are still shaking hands with the devil, instead of sanctifying themselves and calling upon the Lord and doing his work, which He has commanded us and put into our hands to do. When I think upon this subject, I want the tongues of sev[ere] thunders to wake up the people. Can the fathers be saved without us? No.

Can we be saved without them? No. And if we do not wake up and cease to long after the things of this earth, we will find that we as individuals will go down to Hell, although the Lord will preserve a people unto himself.

"Now we are ready to give endowments. Do you have any feelings for those who have died without hearing the gospel? The spirit was awakened in the people in the North. When we gave the word that we should do no more work in the Endowment House, they came to us crying and pleading to be baptized for their dead. What else could they do? They can come here and do the work for their dead and put these poor prisoners on the ground where they will be free. Do we realize this? As long as we tarry here, we are subject to the world, but now go to, like men and women, and say, 'We will embrace the truth and enter into the covenants of God and carry them out.' Then the bonds are broken and the hearts of the people are united in the Father.

"Perhaps Brethren and Sisters you will not get my meaning, but now go to work and let those infernal holes in the ground alone, and let the Gentiles alone, who would destroy us if they had the power. You are running after them and some of our Brethren are putting their wives and daughters into their society and will go to the devil with them too, if they do not look out. I would not have a dollar on the earth if I had to get it there. It has been the kingdom of God with me, and what I have I have got in this kingdom. Well, now some of the elders are running after these holes in the ground, and I see men here before me in this house that have no right to be here. They are as corrupt in their hearts as they can be, and we take them by the hand and call them Brother. You will go to Hell, lots of you, unless you repent. You may think this is plain talk. It is not as plain as you will find by and By. You will go to the gates of Heaven, and Jesus will say, 'I never knew you.' While you have been saying your prayers and going to your meeting and [are] as corrupt in your hearts as man can be. You had better stop now and repent of your sins and sin no more, while their is yet time, and before the doors are closed against you. I want to awake you up and if I had the power to lift the veil from your eyes and let you see things as they are, you would be astonished not but what there are a great many of the people as good as they know how to be.

"Now I will say bless the people that they may do better. But show some of the elders of Israel, according to their present conduct, a dollar on one side and Eternal Life on the other, and I fear they would choose the dollar. We are now prepared to attend to baptizing and giving endowments and shall appoint Tuesdays and Wednesdays for baptisms, and Thursdays and Fridays for endowments and sealings, as a standing appointment for the present. God Bless you. Amen."

I do not know whether the people are satisfied with the services of the dedication of the Temple or not. I am not half satisfied and I never expect to be satisfied until the devil is whipped and driven from off the face of the earth.

In the last remark the President made he struck the pulpit with a hickory cane, filled with knots, with such power that he buried three of the knots into the solid wood that they may remain there for a generation, if they are not filled up. (*Wilford Woodruff's Journal,* 7:316–20; January 1, 1877)

Wilford Woodruff performed the first 141 baptisms for the dead in the St. George Temple.

Performs Ordinances for Many "Choice Spirits"

Shortly after this temple was dedicated in 1877, Wilford Woodruff was visited by the spirits of several great American patriots, who requested him to perform vicarious ordinances for them in the temple. President Ezra Taft Benson wrote, "After he became president of the Church, President Wilford Woodruff declared that 'those men who laid the foundation of this American government were the best spirits the God of heaven could find on the face of the earth. They were choice spirits . . . [and]were inspired of the Lord'" ("Our Divine Constitution," Ensign, *November 1987, 6).*

On August 21, 1877, President Woodruff was baptized as proxy by John D. T. McCallister for the fifty signers of the Declaration of Independence and fifty other prominent men of the seventeenth and eighteenth centuries. President Woodruff wrote:

We have labored in the St. George Temple since January, and we have done all we could there; and the Lord has stirred up our minds, and many things have been revealed to us concerning the dead. President Young has said to us, and it is verily so, [that] if the dead could, they would speak in language [as] loud as ten thousand thunders, calling upon the servants of God to rise up and build Temples, magnify their calling, and redeem their dead. This doubtless sounds strange to those present who believe not the faith and doctrine of the Latter-day Saints; but when we get to the spirit world, we will find out that all that God has revealed is true . . . I feel to say little else to the Latter-day Saints, wherever and whenever I have the opportunity of speaking to them, than to call upon them to build these temples now under way, to hurry them up to completion. The dead will be after you. They will seek after you, as they have after us in St. George. They called upon us, knowing that we held the keys and power to redeem them.

I will here say, before closing, that two weeks before I left St. George, the spirits of the dead gathered around me, wanting to know why we did not redeem them. Said they, "You have had the use of the Endowment House for a number of years, and yet nothing has ever been done for us. We laid the foundation of the government you now enjoy, and we never apostatized from it, but we remained true to it and were faithful to God." These were the signers of the Declaration of Independence, and they waited on me for two days and two nights. I thought it very singular, that notwithstanding so much work had been done, and yet nothing had been done for them. The thought never entered my heart, from the fact, I suppose, that heretofore our minds were reaching after our more immediate friends and relatives. I straightway went into the baptismal font [in the temple] and called upon brother McCallister to baptize me for the signers of the Declaration of Independence, and fifty other eminent men, making one hundred in all, including John Wesley, Columbus, and others. (*Journal of Discourses,* 19:229)

President Woodruff noted the events of August 21 in his journal in these words:

It was a very interesting day. I felt thankful that we had the privilege and the power to administer for the worthy dead, especially for the signers of the Declaration of Independence, that inasmuch as they laid the foundation of our government, that we could do as much for them as they had done for us. (*Wilford Woodruff's Journal,* 7:369; August 21, 1877)

Years later, President Woodruff commented in general conference:

Brother Cannon has been laying before you something with regard to the nation in which we live and what has been said concerning it. I am going to bear my testimony to this assembly, if I never do it again in my life, that those men who laid the foundation of this American government and signed the Declaration of Independence were the best spirits the God of heaven could find on the face of the earth. They were choice spirits, not wicked men. General Washington and all the men that labored for the purpose were inspired of the Lord.

Another thing I am going to say here, because I have a right to say it. Every one of those men that signed the Declaration of Independence with General Washington, called upon me, as an Apostle of the Lord Jesus Christ, in the Temple at St. George, two consecutive nights and demanded at my hands that I should go forth and attend to the ordinances of the House of God for them.

Men are here, I believe, that know of this, Brothers J. D. T. McAllister, David H. Cannon, and James G. Bleak. Brother McAllister baptized me for all those men, and then I told these brethren that it was their duty to go into the Temple and labor until they had got endowments for all of them. They did it. Would those spirits have called upon me, as an elder in Israel, to perform that work if they had not been noble spirits before God? They would not.

I bear this testimony, because it is true. The Spirit of God bore record to myself and the Brethren, while we were laboring in that way. (President Wilford Woodruff, in Conference Report, April 1898, 89–90)

A Period of Reformation

The completion of the Historian's Office [in Salt Lake City in 1856] was followed by the dedication of the Endowment House on October 2. The leading men of the Church met at the baptismal font where the dedicatory prayer was offered by Heber C. Kimball. Elder Woodruff wrote: "It was full of sublimity and prophecy, which found its fulfillment in the history of the font and the building." It would be difficult even to estimate the sacred influence which that building has exercised upon the lives of untold thousands, who felt themselves within its sacred precincts in the presence of their God. The purity that went out from that sacred house into the lives of those who were married there has been the guiding star and the savior of thousands of men and women in the Church. How strange, how remarkable, that a place with such sacred and uplifting influence should be made the object of vicious attacks by those who were the enemies of the Church and its persecutors!

The completion of the font signalized the importance of the so-called Reformation in the Church, which began in that year. President Young entered the font and baptized his counselors, Heber C. Kimball, and Jedediah M. Grant. Later Elder Woodruff and others were baptized; and the privilege extended to all the Saints throughout the Church to renew their covenants. There was a spirit of trouble brewing; a growing opposition throughout the United States toward the Saints was felt by the leaders, who were impressed by the spirit of reform. It was important that the people should be so upright and chaste in their lives that the Lord should have no occasion to punish them for their shortcomings. It was a time of revival in the observance of the duties and the ordinances in the Church. The people were called upon to repent. Questions touching their morals and the manner of their worship were put to the people, both in public places and in their homes. The people generally were asked to renew their covenants by baptism.

An excerpt from the journal of Elder Woodruff illustrates something of the spirit of those times. After explaining to a certain individual that he considered it a privilege to be re-baptized, the man professed his immunity from sin.

"In all the trials incident to the pilgrimage and pioneer life, have you never sworn nor used bad language?"

"No sir," was the prompt reply.

"Have you never broken the Sabbath day?"

"No sir," came the quick response.

"Have you never cheated your neighbor in trade?"

"No sir," thundered the unrepentant man.

"Then, for heavens sake, go off and do something. You are the only perfect man I ever saw, and hope never to see another in this life."

Subsequent events, however, proved that the man who was so self-assertive was the very sort of an individual who was greatly in need of repentance. (*Wilford Woodruff, His Life and Labors,* 372–73)

Organization of the Genealogical Society

President Wilford Woodruff was always very concerned with the work for the dead. In 1894, the Genealogical Society of Utah was organized under his direction. In that same year, President Woodruff announced important matters that the Lord had revealed relating to family sealings:

We want the Latter-day Saints from this time to trace their genealogies as far as they can, and to be sealed to their fathers and mothers. Have children sealed to their parents, and run this chain through as far as you can get it. . . . This is the will of the Lord to this people, and I think when you come to reflect upon it you will find it to be true. . . .

The fathers of this people will embrace the gospel. It is my duty to honor my father who begot me in the flesh. It is your duty to do the same. When you do this, the Spirit of God will be with you. And we shall continue this work, the Lord adding light to that which we have already received. . . . There are men in this congregation who wish to be adopted [sealed] to me. I say to them today, if they can hear me, Go and be adopted [sealed] to your fathers, and save your fathers, and stand at the head of your father's house, as saviors upon Mount Zion, and God will bless you in this. This is what I want to say, and what I want carried out in our temples. . . . I have had a great anxiety over this matter. I have had a great desire that I might live to deliver these principles to the Latter-day Saints, for they are true. They are one step forward in the work of the ministry and in the work of the endowments in these temples of our God. . . . I have gone to work with the assistance of my friends and redeemed my father's and my mother's house. When I inquired of the Lord how I could redeem my dead, while I was in St. George, not having any of my family there, the Lord told me to call upon the Saints in St. George and let them officiate for me in that temple, and it should be acceptable unto him. . . . This is a revelation to us. We can help one another in these matters. (*Discourses of Wilford Woodruff,* 157–59)

God Will Stand by Us Despite the Work of the Adversary

In a letter written to President John Taylor and the Quorum of the Twelve Apostles, dated September 15, 1879, Elder Wilford Woodruff stated: "The devil is making a hard struggle to stop the building of temples, and the work of God, and the wicked are helping him, but, brethren, God reigns and will stand by you to the end" (Wilford Woodruff, His Life and Labors, 528).

Chapter 7

Personal Tests and Trials

Baptized in Ice and Snow

Of his baptism, the last day of the year in 1833, Wilford wrote, "The snow was about three feet deep, the day was cold, and the water was mixed with ice and snow, yet I did not feel the cold" ("Wilford Woodruff 1807–1898," Friend, *March 1980, 34).*

Walks Sixty Miles in One Day

On one occasion, while on a mission to Arkansas and Tennessee, Wilford and his companion walked sixty miles from sunrise until ten o'clock at night "without a morsel of food of any kind." During his missions to England, Elder

Woodruff's faith and hard work resulted in a remarkable number of baptisms—several hundred were performed personally by this valiant leader and servant ("Wilford Woodruff 1807–1898," Friend, *March 1980, 34).*

Wife Raised from the Dead

On the 23rd of November, my wife, Phoebe, was attacked with a severe headache, which terminated in brain fever. She grew more and more distressed daily as we continued our journey. It was a terrible ordeal for a woman to travel in a wagon over rough roads, afflicted as she was. At the same time our child was also very sick.

The 1st of December was a trying day to my soul. My wife continued to fail, and in the afternoon, about 4 o'clock, she appeared to be struck with death. I stopped my team, and it seemed as though she would breathe her last lying in the wagon. Two of the sisters sat beside her, to see if they could do anything for her in her last moments.

I stood upon the ground, in deep affliction, and meditated. I cried unto the Lord, and prayed that she might live and not be taken from me. I claimed the promises the Lord had made unto me through the prophets and patriarchs, and soon her spirit revived, and I drove a short distance to a tavern and got her into a room and worked over her and her babe all night and prayed to the Lord to preserve her life.

In the morning the circumstances were such that I was under the necessity of removing my wife from the inn, as there was so much noise and confusion at the place that she could not endure it. I carried her out to her bed in the wagon and drove two miles, when I alighted at a house and carried my wife and her bed into it, with a determination to tarry there until she either recovered her health or passed away. This was on Sunday morning, December 2nd.

After getting my wife and things into the house, and wood provided to keep up a fire, I employed my time in taking care of her. It looked as though she had but a short time to live.

She called me to her bedside in the evening and said she felt as though a few moments more would end her existence in this life. She manifested great confidence in the cause she had embraced, and exhorted me to have confidence in God and to keep His commandments.

To all appearances, she was dying. I laid hands upon her and prayed for her, and she soon revived and slept some during the night.

December 3rd found my wife very low. I spent the day in taking care of her, and the following day I returned to Eaton to get some things for her. She seemed to be gradually sinking and in the evening her spirit apparently left her body, and she was dead.

The sisters gathered around her body, weeping, while I stood looking at her in sorrow. The spirit and power of God began to rest upon me, until, for the first time during her sickness, faith filled my soul, although she lay before me as one dead.

I had some oil that was consecrated for my anointing, while in Kirtland. I took it and consecrated it again before the Lord for anointing the sick. I then bowed down before the Lord and prayed for the life of my companion, and I anointed her body with the oil in the name of the Lord. I laid my hands upon her, and in the name of Jesus Christ I rebuked the power of death and the destroyer, and commanded the same to depart from her, and the spirit of life to enter her body.

Her spirit returned to her body, and from that hour she was made whole; and we all felt to praise the name of God, and to trust in Him and to keep His commandments.

While this operation was going on with me (as my wife related afterwards) her spirit left her body, and she saw it lying upon the bed, and the sisters weeping. She looked at them and at me, and upon her babe, and, while gazing upon this scene, two personages came into the room carrying a coffin and told her they had come for her body. One of these messengers informed her that she could have her choice: she might go to rest in the spirit world, or, on one condition, she could have the privilege of returning to her tabernacle and continuing her labors upon the earth. The condition was, if she felt that she could stand by her husband, and with him pass through all the cares, trials, tribulation, and afflictions of life which he would be called to pass through for the gospel's sake unto the end. When she looked at the situation of her husband and child, she said: "Yes, I will do it!"

At the moment that decision was made, the power of faith rested upon me, and when I administered unto her, her spirit entered her tabernacle, and she saw the messengers carry the coffin out at the door.

On the morning of the 6th of December, the Spirit said to me: "Arise, and continue thy journey!" and through the mercy of God my wife was enabled to arise and dress herself and walked to the wagon, and we went on our way rejoicing. (*Leaves from My Journal,* 53–55)

Presides During Serious Crisis

It was a time of grave crisis for the Church when President Wilford Woodruff began his administration as President of the Church. President John Taylor had died in exile, and most of the prominent Church leaders were in prison or were unable to lead effectively because of persecutions. Federal laws not only made it unlawful to practice plural marriage but also prohibited those who did so from voting or running for public office. Utah's admission as a state seemed hopelessly deadlocked. There was legislation that sought to disenfranchise all members of the Church. The Church, as an institution, was disincorporated, tithing funds were seized, and Temple Square and other Church properties were transferred to the United States government. There was a serious attempt by many to actually destroy the entity of The Church of Jesus Christ of Latter-day Saints. Missionary work for the living and temple work for the dead were greatly threatened. (*Presidents of the Church,* Institute Student Manual, 68)

President Wilford Woodruff summarized the year 1889 by writing: "Thus ends the year 1889, and the word of the Prophet Joseph Smith is beginning to be fulfilled that the whole nation would turn against Zion and make war upon the Saints. The nation has never been filled so full of lies against the Saints as today. 1890 will be an important year with the Latter-day Saints and [the] American nation" (Wilford Woodruff's Journal, *9:74; December 31, 1889).*

Prevented from Attending Wife's Funeral

Years later, while living in Salt Lake City, Wilford Woodruff was prevented from attending his own wife's funeral, due to the persecution from the anti-plural marriage acts.

In October, he received word that his wife Phoebe was in poor health and he therefore hastened home to Salt Lake City, where he arrived on the 5th of November. He remained, however, in seclusion in his home and neighborhood. On the 10th of November, she died. He was greatly affected by her death and painfully humiliated by the circumstance under which her funeral was held. He stood concealed in the Historian's Office as he watched the funeral procession pass by on its way to the city of the dead. "I am," said he, "passing through a strange chapter in the history of my life. Persecution is raging against the Latter-day Saints. I hope I may prove true and faithful to the end and that I may join her in the Celestial kingdom of God and have part in the first resurrection." (*Wilford Woodruff, His Life and Labors,* 556)

Daughter Dies During His Mission to England

"Great sorrow struck on July 17, when two-year-old

Sarah Emma died" (Wilford Woodruff's Journal, *1:371; November 28, 1839). The next day, the heartsick Phoebe wrote an anguished and tender letter to the absent father. Its words eloquently reveal her pain and pathos, as well as the remarkable faith of these stalwart women who lived without their husbands on the edge of civilization, helping to build a new gathering place for the Saints of God.*

My dear Wilford, what will be your feelings, when I say that yesterday I was called to witness the departure of our little Sarah Emma from this world. Yes, she is gone. The relentless hand of death has snatched her from my embrace. But Ah! She was too lovely, too kind, too affectionate to live in this wicked world. When looking on her, I have often thought how I should feel to part with her. I thought I could not live without her especially in the absence of my companion. But she has gone. The Lord hath taken her home to himself for some wise purpose.

It is a trial to me, but the Lord hath stood by me in a wonderful manner. I can see and feel and [know] that he has taken her home and will take better care of her than I possibly could for a little while, until I shall go and meet her. Yes, Wilford we have one little angel in heaven and I think it likely her spirit has visited you before this time.

It is hard living without her. She used to call her poor Pa Pa and putty papa many times in a day. She left a kiss for her papa with me just before she died. She ate her dinner as well as usual Thursday. Was taken about four o'clock with a prestness [*sic*] for breath. The elders laid hands upon her and anointed her a number of times, but the next day her spirit took its flight from this to another world, without a groan.

Today Wilford and I with quite a number of friends accompanying us came over to Commerce to pay our last respects to our little darling in seeing her decently buried. She had no relative to follow her to the grave or to shed a tear for her but her ma and little Wilford. . . . I have just been to take a pleasing melancholy walk to Sarah's grave; she lies alone in peace. I can say that the Lord gave and the Lord hath taken away and blessed be the name of the *Lord.* (*Wilford Woodruff's Journal,* 1:542; October 26, 1840)

Margaret Smoot also wrote a letter to Wilford that day, in which she enclosed a poem about Sarah and asked him to accept it "from one who had every feeling but that of a parent for your departed Sarah" (*Wilford Woodruff's Journal,* 1:541; October 26, 1840). With the aid of many good friends, Phoebe endured the loss of Sarah Emma (*Men with a Mission, 1837–1841: The Quorum of the Twelve Apostles in the British Isles,* 287).

Learns from Trials to Have God As His Friend

At that time, he was called upon to mourn the demise of his beloved brother Philo. A few months prior to his death, Philo dreamed that an angel from heaven was going through the streets of the town with a roll containing a list of those who should die during the year in that town. The angel approached Philo and unfolded to him the roll, at the same time he informed him that on November 27 there would be a funeral at his father's house. Philo recorded the dream in his journal. On the very day named by the angel, his own funeral occurred at his father's home. The fulfillment of this strange dream made a lasting impression on Wilford's mind.

The year following, another very remarkable circumstance occurred which was equally impressive to his thoughtful and spiritual mind. He writes: "I was called to sit up for the night with the remains of a young man named Henry Miller. He had been very wicked and profane. The day before his death, he attended a celebration of the nation's birthday, July 4th. The boy's father, who was a religious, God-fearing man, reproved the son for his profanity and wickedness. Shortly after this, he and his father were on their way to the field to get some hay, when there suddenly arose a heavy shower, accompanied by thunder and lightning. Henry made sport of the roaring elements and mocked God in the thunder. The next moment, while standing by his father's side, he was struck by a thunderbolt from heaven. I attended his funeral. The circumstances of his death made a lasting impression on me."

Like many for whom there is in store a remarkable religious future, Wilford was called to suffer financial reverses [so] that he might learn how uncertain are the goods of this world and that he might feel the full force of that divine fiat: "Cursed is he that trusteth in riches; cursed is he that trusteth in man, or maketh flesh his arm." He had earned considerable money while running the flour mill for his Aunt Helen, but lost much of it by lending it to an unprincipled man and by helping others who were unable to repay him. These peculiar experiences, temporal and spiritual, fortunes and misfortunes, accidents and trials among people away from his own home filled his soul with grave reflections and brought him to take a stand relative to his own future course in life. He was high-minded, had no vices or bad habits, and his standard of purity and excellence was so high that he never indulged in light-mindedness or in trifling recreations. To him they were grevious sins in the sight of God; and he believed, with the Prophet Joseph, that they should be eschewed. He was constantly striving for a higher plane upon which he might firmly plant his feet. (*Wilford Woodruff, His Life and Labors,* 25–26; punctuation standardized)

Bids Tearful Farewell to the Prophet Joseph Smith

This [mission to the Eastern States] was the last mission the Prophet ever gave to the Twelve Apostles in this dispensation. He wished none of us to remain by him except Willard Richards. Apostle John Taylor was later required to remain and take charge of the printing and publications. The Prophet then turned to me and said: "Brother Woodruff, I want you to go, and if you do not you will die." His words rested with mighty weight upon me when he spoke, and I have often thought since, in contemplation of the awful tragedy of his and Hyrum's martyrdom, how truly his words would have been verified had I remained. Elder Taylor barely escaped. Willard Richards escaped the bullets altogether. He escaped, as was written of him later, "without even a hole in his robe." I took the parting hand of Hyrum and Joseph, at their own dwellings. Joseph stood in the entry of his door when I took his hand to bid him farewell. Brother J. M. Grant was with me. As he took me by the hand, he said: "Brother Woodruff, you are about to start upon your mission." I answered, "Yes." He looked me steadily in the eye for a time without speaking a word; he looked as though he would penetrate my very soul, and at the same time seemed unspeakably sorrowful as if weighed down by a foreboding of something dreadful. He finally spoke in a mournful voice: "God bless you, Brother Woodruff; go in peace." I turned and left him with a sorrowful heart, partaking of the same spirit which rested upon him. This was the last time I ever saw his face or heard his voice again—in the flesh. (*Wilford Woodruff, His Life and Labors,* 204–5)

Chapter 8

Following the Promptings of the Spirit

Governed and Controlled by the Spirit

I never disobeyed that Spirit but once in my life; I did it then through the urgency of other persons, and it nearly cost me my life. I have been acquainted with this Spirit. It was not the blow of trumpets nor thunder and lightning; it was the still small voice to me. All the way from my boyhood, I have been governed and controlled by that Spirit. My missions have been by that Spirit of revelation. I was told to go to [the] Fox Islands by that same still small voice. In the time of the great apostasy in Kirtland, the Spirit of the Lord said to me, "Get you a partner and go to [the] Fox Islands." I knew no more

[of] what was in Fox Islands than what was in Kolob. I went there, however, baptized a hundred, and brought them up to Zion with me. It was upon that Island where I received a letter from Joseph Smith, telling me that I was called by revelation to fill the place of one of the Twelve who had fallen. You will see it in the Doctrine and Covenants. That thing was revealed to me before I received the letter from Joseph Smith, but I did not feel disposed to tell it to any mortal man, for I knew it was my duty to keep such things to myself. Through all my life and labors, whenever I have been told to do anything by the Spirit of the Lord, I have always found it good to do it. I have been preserved by that power. (Wilford Woodruff, in Conference Report, April 1898, 30–31)

Following the Promptings of the Spirit Saves His Farm

After attending a large annual conference in Salt Lake City, and, having a good deal of business to attend to, I was somewhat weary. And, at the close of the conference, I thought I would repair to my home and have a rest.

As I went into the yard, the Spirit said to me, "Take your team and go to the farm," which is some three miles south of the Tabernacle.

As I was hitching the horse to the wagon, Mrs. Woodruff asked where I was going.

I said, "To the farm."

"What for?" she asked.

"I do not know," I replied; but when I arrived there I found out.

The creek had overflowed, broken through my ditch, surrounded my home, and filled my barnyard and pig pen. . . . Through my own exertions, I soon turned it and prevented much damage that might have occurred had I not obeyed the voice of the Spirit.

This same Spirit of revelation has been manifested to many of my brethren in their labors in the kingdom of God. (*Leaves from My Journal,* 89)

Moves His Carriage Just in Time

In 1848, after my return to Winter Quarters from our pioneer journey, I was appointed by the presidency of the Church to take my family and go to Boston, to gather up the remnant of the Saints and lead them to the valleys of the mountains.

While on my way east, I put my carriage into the yard of one of the brethren in Indiana, and Brother Orson Hyde set his wagon by the side of mine, and not more than two feet from it.

Dominicus Carter, of Provo, and my wife and four children were with me. My wife, one child, and I went to bed in the carriage, the rest sleeping in the house.

I had been in bed but a short time when a voice said to me: "Get up, and move your carriage."

It was not thunder, lightning, or an earthquake, but the still, small voice of the Spirit of God—the Holy Ghost.

I told my wife I must get up and move my carriage. She asked: "What for?"

I told her I did not know, only the Spirit told me to do it.

I got up and moved my carriage several rods, and set it by the side of the house.

As I was returning to bed, the same spirit said to me, "Go and move your mules from that oak tree," which was about one hundred yards north of our carriage.

I moved them to a young hickory grove and tied them up. I then went to bed.

In thirty minutes a whirlwind caught the tree to which my mules had been fastened, broke it off near the ground and carried it one hundred yards, sweeping away two fences in its course, and laid it prostrate through that yard where my carriage stood, and the top limbs hit my carriage as it was.

In the morning I measured the trunk of the tree which fell where my carriage had stood, and I found it to be five feet in circumference. It came within a foot of Brother Hyde's wagon, but did not touch it.

Thus, by obeying the revelation of the Spirit of God to me, I saved my life and the lives of my wife and child, as well as my animals. (*Leaves from My Journal*, 88)

Warned by the Spirit Not to Board Steamer

When I got back to Winter Quarters from the pioneer journey [1847], President Young said to me, "Brother Woodruff, I want you to take your wife and children and go to Boston and stay there until you can gather every saint of God in New England and Canada and send them up to Zion."

I did as he told me. It took me two years to gather up everybody, and I brought up the rear with a company (there were about one hundred of them). We arrived at

Pittsburgh one day at sundown. We did not want to stay there, so I went to the first steamboat that was going to leave.

I saw the captain and engaged passage for us on that steamer. I had only just done so when the Spirit said to me, and that, too, very strongly, "Don't go aboard that steamer, nor your company." Of course, I went and spoke to the captain, and told him I had made up my mind to wait.

Well, that ship started, and had only got five miles down the river when it took fire, and three hundred persons were burned to death or drowned. If I had not obeyed that Spirit, and had gone on that steamer with the rest of the company, you can see what the result would have been. (*The Discourses of Wilford Woodruff*, 294–95)

Disobedience Nearly Costs Him His Life

I will now give an example from my own experience of the result of not obeying the voice of the Spirit.

Some years since I had part of my family living in Randolph, Rich County, I was there on a visit, with my team, in the month of December.

One Monday morning my monitor, the Spirit watching over me, said: "Take your team and go home to Salt Lake City."

When I named it to my family, who were at Randolph, they urged me strongly to stop longer.

Through their persuasion I stayed until Saturday morning, with the Spirit continually prompting me to go home. I then began to feel ashamed to think that

I had not obeyed the whisperings of the Spirit to me before.

I took my team and started early on Saturday morning. When I arrived at Woodruff, the Bishop urged me to stop until Monday and he would go with me.

I told him, "No, I have tarried too long already."

I drove on sprightly, and when within fifteen miles of Wasatch, a furious storm overtook me, the wind blowing heavily in my face.

In fifteen minutes I could not see any road whatever, and knew not how or where to guide my horses.

I left my lines loosely on my animals, went inside my wagon, tied down my cover, and committed my life and guidance into the hands of the Lord, trusting to my horses to find the way, as they had twice before passed over that road.

I prayed to the Lord to forgive my sin in not obeying the voice of the Spirit to me, and implored Him to preserve my life.

My horses brought me onto the Wasatch station at 9 o'clock in the evening, with the hubs of my wagon dragging in the snow.

I got my horses under cover, and had to remain there until next Monday night, with the snow six feet deep on the level, and still snowing.

It was with great difficulty at last that I saved the lives of my horses by getting them into a box car and taking them to Ogden; while, if I had obeyed the revelation of the Spirit of God to me, I should have traveled to Salt Lake City over a good road, without any storm.

As I have received the good and the evil, the fruits

of obedience and disobedience, I think I am justified in exhorting all my young friends to always obey the whisperings of the Spirit of God, and they will always be safe. (*Leaves from My Journal*, 90–91)

Sees the Prophet Heal Many in Nauvoo

While I was living in this cabin in the old barracks, we experienced a day of God's power with the Prophet Joseph. It was a very sickly time, and Joseph had given up his home in Commerce to the sick and had a tent pitched in his door-yard and was living in that himself. The large number of Saints who had been driven out of Missouri were flocking into Commerce; but had no homes to go into and were living in wagons, in tents, and on the ground. Many, therefore, were sick through the exposure they were subjected to. Brother Joseph had waited on the sick, until he was worn out and nearly sick himself.

On the morning of the 22nd of July, 1839, he arose, reflecting upon the situation of the Saints of God in their persecutions and afflictions, and he called upon the Lord in prayer, and the power of God rested upon him mightily, and as Jesus healed all the sick around Him in His day, so Joseph, the Prophet of God, healed all around on this occasion. He healed all in his house and dooryard; then, in company with Sidney Rigdon and several of the Twelve, he went among the sick lying on the bank of the river, and he commanded them in a loud voice, in the name of Jesus Christ, to come up and be made whole, and they were all healed. When he healed all that were sick on the east side of the river, they crossed the Mississippi River in a ferryboat to the west side, to Montrose, where we were. The first house they went into was President Brigham Young's. He was sick on his bed at the time. The Prophet went into his house and healed him, and they all came out together. As they were passing by my door, Brother Joseph said: "Brother Woodruff, follow me." These were the only words spoken by any of the company from the time they left Brother Brigham's house till we crossed the public square, and entered Brother Fordham's house. Brother Fordham had been dying for an hour, and we expected each minute would be his last.

I felt the power of God that was overwhelming His Prophet.

When we entered the House, Brother Joseph walked up to Brother Fordham, and took him by the right hand; in his left hand he held his hat.

He saw that Brother Fordham's eyes were glazed, and that he was speechless and unconscious.

After taking hold of his hand, he looked down into the dying man's face and said: "Brother Fordham, do you not know me?" At first he made no reply; but we could all see the effect of the Spirit of God resting upon him.

He again said: "Elijah, do you not know me?"

With a low whisper, Brother Fordham answered, "Yes!"

The Prophet then said, "Have you not faith to be healed?" The answer, which was a little plainer than before, was: "I am afraid it is too late. If you had come sooner, I think I might have been."

He had the appearance of a man waking from sleep. It was the sleep of death.

Joseph then said: "Do you believe that Jesus is the Christ?"

"I do, Brother Joseph," was the response.

Then the Prophet of God spoke with a loud voice, as in the majesty of the Godhead: "Elijah, I command you, in the name of Jesus of Nazareth, to arise and be made whole!"

The words of the Prophet were not like the words of man, but like the voice of God. It seemed to me that the house shook from its foundation.

Elijah Fordham leaped from his bed like a man raised from the dead. A healthy color came to his face, and life was manifested in every act.

His feet were done up in Indian meal poultices. He kicked them off his feet, scattered the contents, and then called for his clothes and put them on. He asked for a bowl of bread and milk, and ate it; then put on his hat and followed us into the street, to visit others who were sick.

The unbeliever may ask: "Was there not deception in this?"

If there is any deception in the mind of the unbeliever, there was certainly none with Elijah Fordham, the dying man, nor with those who were present with him, for in a few minutes more he would have been in the spirit world, had he not been rescued. Through the blessing of God, he lived up till 1880, in which year he died in Utah, while all who were with him on that occasion, with the exception of one, are in the spirit world.

Among the number, were Joseph and Hyrum Smith, Sidney Rigdon, Brigham Young, Heber C. Kimball, George A. Smith, Parley P. Pratt and Orson Pratt. Wilford Woodruff is the only one living who was present at the time, and he will soon mingle with those who have gone. (*Leaves from My Journal*, 62–66)

Later, commenting on this miraculous day of healing, President Woodruff wrote:

It is very seldom that I have known the power of the priesthood made manifest upon the children of men in our [time] to a very great degree, but in some instances it was manifest, as in the case of the prophet Joseph, at the time his [house] was full of the sick and dying, and his dooryard; and they were strewed along the bank of the river for two miles and Joseph rose up and shook himself like an old lion, and commenced at his own tent door and healed all the people who were not dead on both sides of the river, by the power of God. His voice was as the voice of God and the earth almost trembled under his feet as he commanded the sick to arise and be made whole. (*Wilford Woodruff's Journal*, 5:23; February 17, 1857)

Casts Out an Evil Spirit

December 1st. . . After retiring to rest at night, I was called upon by Brother Meeks to go with him to lay hands upon his wife who was possessed with a devil. I went with him to his house and found his wife foaming in great agony. I laid hands upon her and rebuked the devil and he came out of her and she soon fell asleep and I returned home. . . If I had judged from outward appearances, I should have thought the devil followed me home and entered into our cat, for she made the most awful noise through the night I ever heard. I also had a disagreeable dream . . . which I considered to be from the devil. I met in council with the Twelve in evening. (*Wilford Woodruff's Journal,* 2:140; December 1, 1841)

Joseph Smith Appears to Him

I had a peculiar dream last night, one that is unutterable and cannot be written, for I cannot comprehend it all myself. I was called to hold the keys of the kingdom of God in all the world with the quorum of the Twelve and traveled with them over much of the world, and finally traveled through many countries alone. . . . When I got through, I saw many things I cannot write, but in the end Br. Joseph Smith assisted me to come into the place where he was and pointed out my work, portion, and labor. I immediately entered into the duties assigned me. (*Wilford Woodruff's Journal,* 2:478–79; November 1, 1844)

I also had another dream. [I] was in the presence of Brother Joseph Smith . . . conversing about his death. [I] told him I felt bad about it and if I had known he would have been taken away so soon, I should have conversed more with him and asked him more questions. Said it was not his fault that I did not. Speaking of my work and duties, [he] said I had better get a dozen to help me. (*Wilford Woodruff's Journal,* 2:479; November 1, 1844)

"Joseph Smith Visited Me after His Death"

One morning, while we were at Winter Quarters, Brother Brigham Young said to me and the brethren that he had had a visitation the night previous from Joseph Smith. I asked him what he said to him. He replied that Joseph had told him to tell the people to labor to obtain the Spirit of God; that they needed that to sustain them and to give them power to go through their work on the earth.

Now I will give you a little of my experience in this line. Joseph Smith visited me a great deal after his death, and taught me many important principles. The last time he visited me was while I was in a storm at sea. I was going on my last mission to preside in England. My companions were Brother Leonard W. Hardy, Brother Milton Holmes, Brother Dan Jones, and another brother, and my wife and two other women. We had been traveling three days and nights in a heavy gale, and were being driven backwards. Finally I asked my companions to come into the cabin with me, and I told them to pray that the Lord would change the wind. I had no fears of being lost; but I did not like the idea of being driven back to New York, as I wanted to go on my journey. We all offered the same prayer, both men and women; and when we got through we stepped on to the deck and in less than a minute it was as though a man had taken a sword and cut that gale through, and you might have thrown a muslin handkerchief out and it would not have moved it. The night following this, Joseph and Hyrum visited me, and the Prophet laid before me a great many things. Among other things, he told me to get the Spirit of God; that all of us needed it. He also told me what the Twelve Apostles would be called to go through on the earth before the coming of the Son of Man, and what the reward of their labors would be; but all that was taken from me, for some reason. Nevertheless, I know it was most glorious, although much would be required at our hands.

Joseph Smith continued visiting myself and others up to a certain time, and then it stopped. The last time I saw him was in heaven. In the night vision, I saw him at the door of the temple in heaven. He came and spoke to me. He said he could not stop to talk with me because he was in a hurry. The next man I met was Father Smith; he could not talk with me because he was in a hurry. I met half a dozen brethren who had held high positions on earth, and none of them could stop to talk with me because they were in a hurry. I was much astonished. By and by, I saw the Prophet again, and I got the privilege to ask him a question. "Now," said I, "I want to know why you are in a hurry. I have been in a hurry all through my life; but I expected my hurry would be over when I got into the kingdom of heaven, if I ever did." Joseph said: "I will tell you, Brother Woodruff. Every dispensation that has had the Priesthood on the earth and has gone into the Celestial Kingdom, has had a certain amount of work to do to prepare to go to the earth with the Savior when He goes to reign on the earth. Each dispensation has had ample time to do this work. We have not. We are the last dispensation, and so much work has to be done, and we need to be in a hurry in order to accomplish it." Of course, that was satisfactory to me, but it was new doctrine to me. ("Discourse," *Deseret Weekly*, 7 November 1896, 642–43)

"She Laid Down Her Crutch and Never Used It After"

Mary Pitt . . . was something like the lame man who lay at the gate of the temple called "Beautiful," at Jerusalem—she had not been able to walk a step for fourteen years, and confined to her bed nearly half that time. She had no strength in her feet and ankles and could only move about a little with a crutch or holding on to a chair. She wished to be baptized. Brother Pitt [Mary's brother] and myself took her in our arms, and carried her into the water, and I baptized her. When she came out of the water, I confirmed her. She said she wanted to be healed and she believed she had faith enough to be healed. I had had experience enough in this church to know that it required a good deal of faith to heal a person who had not walked a step for fourteen years. I told her that according to her faith it should be unto her. It so happened that on the day after she was baptized, Brother Richards and President Brigham Young came down to see me. We met at Brother Kington's. Sister Mary Pitt was there also. I told President Young what Sister Pitt wished, and that she believed she had faith enough to be healed. We prayed for her and laid hands upon her. Brother Young was mouth and commanded her to be made whole. She laid down her crutch and never used it after, and the next day she walked three miles. (*Journal of Discourses*, 15:344)

Heals Children at Joseph's Command

A man of the world, knowing of the miracles which had been performed, came to [Joseph Smith] and asked him if he would not go and heal two twin children of his, about five months old, who were both lying sick nigh unto death.

They were some two miles from Montrose, [Iowa].

The Prophet said he could not go; but, after pausing some time, he said he would send someone to heal them; and he turned to me and said: "You go with the man and heal his children." He took a red silk handkerchief out of his pocket and gave it to me, and told me to wipe their faces with the handkerchief when I administered to them, and they should be healed. He also said unto me: "As long as you will keep that handkerchief, it shall remain a league between you and me."

I went with the man, and did as the Prophet commanded me, and the children were healed.

I have possession of the handkerchief unto this day." (*Leaves from My Journal,* 65)

The Ministering of Angels

Commenting on the subject of the ministering of angels, President Wilford Woodruff said:

One of the Apostles said to me years ago, "Brother Woodruff, I have prayed for a long time for the Lord to send the administration of an angel to me. I have had a great desire for this, but I have never had my prayers answered." I said to him that if he were to pray a thousand years to the God of Israel for that gift it would not be granted unless the Lord had a motive in sending an angel to him. I told him that the Lord never did nor never will send an angel to anybody merely to gratify the desire of the individual to see an angel. If the Lord sends an angel to anyone, He sends him to perform a work that cannot be performed, only by the administration of an angel. I said to him that these were my views. The Lord had sent angels to men from the creation of the world, at different times, but always with a message or with something to perform that could not be performed without [the appearance]. I rehearsed to him different times when angels appeared to men. Of course I referred to the angel visiting Joseph Smith. The Revelator John said that in the last days an angel would fly in the midst of heaven, having the everlasting Gospel to preach to them that dwelt on the earth. The reason it required an angel to do this work was the [that] gospel and the priesthood had been taken from among men. Hence, God had to restore it again. . . .

I have never prayed for the visitation of an angel, but I have had the ministration of an angel several times in my life. . . .

I traveled thousands of miles and preached the gospel as a Priest, and, as I have said to congregations before, the Lord sustained me and made manifest His power in the defense of my life as much while I held that office as He has done while I have held the office of an Apostle. The Lord sustains any man that holds a portion of the priesthood, whether he is a Priest, an elder, a seventy or an Apostle if he magnifies his calling and does his duty. ("Discourse," *Deseret Weekly News,* 641)

Personal Revelation—a Gift of the Spirit

President Wilford Woodruff taught the following about revelation:

What is revelation? The testimony of the Father and Son. How many of you have had revelation? How many of you have had the Spirit of God whisper unto you—the still small voice? I would have been in the spirit world a great many years ago if I had not followed the promptings of the still small voice. These were the revelations of Jesus Christ, the strongest testimony a man or a woman can have. I have had many testimonies since I have been connected with this church and kingdom. I have been blessed at times with certain gifts and graces, certain revelations and ministrations; but with them all, I have never found anything that I could place more dependency upon than the still small voice of the Holy Ghost. (*Discourses of Wilford Woodruff,* 45)

It is this preknowledge which God has given concerning his work . . . which is one of the chief causes of the strength possessed by the Latter-day Saints. It is the principle of revelation from the head of the church to the church itself—a principle which, in its operation, is not confined to one man or to three men or to twelve men; but is extended to every individual in the Church, in greater or less degree, as each one chooses to avail himself of it. There is an appointed way, however, in which revelation from the Lord for the government of his church is received. There is but one man on the earth, at a time, who holds this power. But every individual member has the privilege of receiving revelation from the Lord for his guidance in his own affairs. (*Discourses of Wilford Woodruff,* 54)

The Lord would not permit me to occupy this position one day of my life unless I was susceptible to the Holy Spirit and to the revelations of God. It is too late in the day for this church to stand without revelation. (*Discourses of Wilford Woodruff,* 57)

Sees the Future of the United States

In his journal entry for January 26, 1880, Wilford Woodruff wrote:

I went to bed filled with prayer and meditation. I fell asleep and slept until about midnight. I awoke. The Lord poured out His spirit upon me and opened the vision of my mind so I could comprehend in a good measure the mind and will of God and His purposes concerning our nation and the inhabitants of Zion. And when the vision of my mind was open to comprehend the situation of our nation, their wickedness, abominations, and corruptions and the judgments of God and the destruction that awaited them, and when I comprehended the great and mighty responsibility which rested upon the Quorum of the Apostles in the sight of God and the heavenly hosts, my head became a fountain of tears and my pillow was wet as with the dews of heaven. And sleep departed from me, and the Lord revealed unto me our duty, even the duty of the Twelve Apostles and all the faithful elders of Israel. (*Wilford Woodruff's Journal,* 7:546; January 26, 1880)

"Get the Spirit of God"

Joseph Smith visited me a great deal after his death, and taught me many important principles. . . . Among other things, he told me to get the Spirit of God; that all of us needed it. . . .

Brigham Young also visited me after his death. . . . And he told me what Joseph Smith had taught him in Winter Quarters, to teach the people to get the Spirit of God. He said, "I want you to teach the people to get the Spirit of God. You cannot build up the kingdom of God without that."

That is what I want to say to the brethren and sisters here today. Every man and woman in this Church should labor to get that Spirit. We are surrounded by these evil spirits that are at war against God and against everything looking to the building up of the kingdom of God; and we need this Holy Spirit to enable us to overcome these influences. I have had the Holy Ghost in my travels. Every man has that has gone out into the vineyard and labored faithfully for the cause of God. I have referred to the administration of angels to myself. What did these angels do? One of them taught me some things relating to the signs that should precede the coming of the Son of Man. Others came and saved my life. What then? They turned and left me. But how is it with the Holy Ghost? The Holy Ghost does not leave me if I do my duty. It does not leave any man who does his duty. We have known this all the way through. Joseph Smith told Brother John Taylor on one occasion to labor to get the Spirit of God, and to follow its dictation, and it would become a principle of revelation within him.

God has blessed me with that, and everything I have done since I have been in this church has been done upon that principle. The Spirit of God has told me what to do, and I have had to follow that. ("Discourse," *The Deseret Weekly*, November 7, 1896, 642–43)

Wilford Woodruff's Testimony

In 1897, President Wilford Woodruff recorded his testimony on a "talking machine." He was the first prophet to ever have his voice recorded. He said:

I bear my testimony that Joseph Smith was a true prophet of God, ordained of God to lay the foundation of his church and kingdom in the last dispensation and fulness of times. I bear my testimony that in the early spring of 1844, in Nauvoo, the Prophet Joseph Smith called the Twelve Apostles together, and he delivered unto them the ordinances of the Church and kingdom of God; and all of the keys and powers that God had bestowed upon him, he sealed upon our heads. He told us we must round up our shoulders and bear off this kingdom or we would be damned. I am the only man now living in the flesh who heard that testimony from his mouth, and I know it is true by the power of God manifest through him. At that meeting, he began to speak about three hours upon the subject of the kingdom. His face was as clear as amber, and he was covered with a power that I had never seen in the flesh before. In all his testimony to us, the power of God was visibly manifest in the Prophet Joseph.

This is my testimony, spoken by myself into a talking machine on this the nineteenth day of March, 1897, in the ninety-first year of my age. Wilford Woodruff. ("Record Transcription," *New Era,* January 1972, 66)

Appendix

This appendix is designed to assist those teaching or studying from the Teachings of Presidents of the Church: Wilford Woodruff *manual. Each chapter in the manual is listed in bold, followed by the section and page number in this book that complements the material in each respective chapter.*

The Life and Ministry of Wilford Woodruff

Chapter 1: The Restoration of the Gospel

Chapter 2: Joseph Smith: Prophet, Seer, and Revelator

Chapter 3: The Dispensation of the Fulness of Times

Chapter 4: The Power and Authority of the Holy Priesthood

Chapter 5: The Holy Ghost and Personal Revelation

Chapter 13: Journals: "Of Far More Worth than Gold"

Chapter 14: Remembering Our Spiritual Heritage

Chapter 15: Living by Faith

Chapter 16: Marriage and Parenthood: Preparing Our Families for Eternal Life

Chapter 17: Temple Work: Turning Our Hearts to Our Families and to the Lord

for Truth (page 35)
2. Labors to Help Redeem the Dead (page 89)
3. Dedication of the St. George Temple (page 90)
4. Performs Ordinances for Many "Choice Spirits" (page 96)
5. A Period of Reformation (page 99)
6. Organization of the Genealogical Society (page 101)
7. God Will Stand by Us Despite the Work of the Adversary (page 102)
8. "Joseph Smith Visited Me After His Death" (page 126)

Chapter 18: Temple Work: Becoming Saviors on Mount Zion

1. Teachings of Robert Mason Help Direct Wilford's Search for Truth (page 35)
2. Labors to Help Redeem the Dead (page 89)
3. Dedication of the St. George Temple (page 90)
4. Performs Ordinances for Many "Choice Spirits" (page 96)
5. A Period of Reformation (page 99)
6. Organization of the Genealogical Society (page 101)
7. God Will Stand by Us Despite the Work of the Adversary (page 122)
8. "Joseph Smith Visited Me After His Death" (page 126)

Chapter 19: Following the Living Prophet

1. A Love for the Words of God (page 84)
2. Bids Tearful Farewell to the Prophet Joseph Smith (page 112)

Chapter 20: Agency: Choosing Life or Death

1. Gains an Understanding of the Purpose of Life (page 30)
2. Commits Himself to the Lord (page 33)
3. Desires the Blessings of Eternity above All Earthly Blessings (page 42)
4. Learns from Trials to Have God as His Friend (page 110)

5. Disobedience Nearly Costs Him His Life (page 119)

Chapter 21: Faithfully Enduring Trials and Opposition

1. Encounters Wild Animals (page 53)
2. Sacrifices Made to Serve (page 70)
3. Baptized in Ice and Snow (page 103)
4. Walks Sixty Miles in One Day (page 103)
5. Wife Raised from the Dead (page 104)
6. Presides During Serious Crisis (page 107)
7. Prevented from Attending Wife's Funeral (page 108)
8. Daughter Dies During His Mission to England (page 108)
9. Learns from Trials to Have God as His Friend (page 110)

Chapter 22: Temporal and Spiritual Labor, "Hand in Hand Together"

1. A Legacy of Hard Work (page 16)
2. Gains an Understanding of the Purpose of Life (page 30)
3. Consecrates His All to the Lord (page 41)
4. Desires the Blessings of Eternity above All Earthly Blessings (page 42)
5. Sacrifices to Help Build the Kingdom of God (page 42)

Chapter 23: "Of One Heart and Mind"

1. Consecrates His All to the Lord (page 41)
2. Generosity of the Apostles (page 71)

Chapter 24: Preparing for the Second Coming of Jesus Christ

1. "Joseph Smith Visited Me After His Death" (page 126)

Sources

Allen, James B., Ronald K. Esplin, and David J. Whittaker. *Men with a Mission, 1837–1841: The Quorum of the Twelve Apostles in the British Isles.* Salt Lake City: Deseret Book, 1992.

Conference Reports of The Church of Jesus Christ of Latter-day Saints. Salt Lake City: The Church of Jesus Christ of Latter-day Saints, 1898 to the present.

Crocheron, Augusta Joyce. *Representative Women of Deseret: A Book of Biographical Sketches to Accompany the Picture Bearing the Same Title.* Salt Lake City: J. C. Graham 7 Co., 1884.

Journal of Discourses. 26 vols. London: Latter-day Saints' Book Depot, 1854–1886.

The Latter-day Saints' Millennial Star. Manchester, Liverpool, and London, England: The Church of Jesus Christ of Latter-day Saints, 1840–1970.

LeBaron, Dale E. "Sacrifice Brings Forth the Blessings of Heaven." *Regional Studies in LDS History: British Isles.* Provo, Utah: Brigham Young University, 1990.

Nibley, Preston. *The Presidents of the Church.* 13th ed. rev. Salt Lake City: Deseret Book, 1974.

Presidents of the Church. Salt Lake City: The Church of Jesus Christ of Latter-day Saints, 2003.

Smith, Joseph Fielding. *Church History and Modern Revelation.* 4 vols. Salt Lake City: The Church of Jesus Christ of Latter-day Saints, 1946–1949.

Times and Seasons. Commerce (later Nauvoo, Illinois), 1839–1846.

Whitney, Orson F. *Life of Heber C. Kimball.* Salt Lake City: Deseret Book, 2001.

———. *Leaves from My Journal: Third Book of the Faith-Promoting Series.* Salt Lake City: Juvenile Instructor Office, 1882.

———. *The Discourses of Wilford Woodruff.* Edited by G. Homer Durham. Salt Lake City: Bookcraft, 1946.

———. *Collected Discourses.* Compiled and edited by Brian H. Stuy. 5 vols. Burbank, Calif.: BHS Publishing, 1886–1898.

———. *Wilford Woodruff, His Life and Labors.* Compiled by Matthias F. Cowley. Salt Lake City: Deseret News, 1916.

———. *Wilford Woodruff's Journal: 1833–1898.* Typescript. Edited by Scott G. Kenney. 9 vols. Midvale, Utah: Signature Books, 1983.

0 26575 79258 4